A **NEW FEMININE EVOLUTIONARY** BOOK

PIONEERING THE PATH TO
PROSPERITY

DISCOVER THE POWER OF TRUE WEALTH & ABUNDANCE

FEATURING
ALEXIS NEELY | TANYA LYNN PALUSO | ALIS MAO
COMPILED BY JANE ASHLEY WITH CONTRIBUTIONS FROM 22 NEW PARADIGM LEADERS

FLOWER OF LIFE PRESS.
Voices of Transformation

PRAISE

"In her signature heart-centered, authentic style, Rima Bonario offers a simple, yet powerfully effective three-step process to shift our relationship with money. Let Rima's deeply intuitive wisdom guide you in transforming your relationship with prosperity and become an expert receiver."

—Jane Simmons Th.D., Author of *You Can't Sleep Through Your Awakening*

"In her diagnosis of money dysmorphia, Alexis Neely hits at a fundamental truth: many individuals are obsessed with money while grossly mis-perceiving the objective reality of it, namely that it is an infinitely renewable resource that has always derived its use value from outside of itself, in what people consider worthwhile. For those who are all-consumed by money and as a result find themselves suffering or bereft in some way, the remedy is deceptively simple: attend to the root of what one really wants and intrinsic values, and then apply limited resources of time, attention, and energy in service of those ends. Neely dares us to discover what it means and looks like for us to enrich and be enriched by others."

—Rebecca

"Lainie Love Dalby is a powerhouse. Her writing is honest, inspiring, potent, clear, fierce, and moving. It's grand work!"

—Virginia Rosenberg

"Mia Luz, mystic, earth goddess, and all-around visionary shares in this poetically written piece her sacred perspective on abundance. Her inspirational tale is one you will read many times to absorb its sheer beauty and grace—it will forever change your relationship with abundance."

—Judy Sorrano

"At the point of complete darkness is the beginning of light. Maribeth Morrissey's life story is a testament of power being forged through authentic vulnerability. Like a sword put through the fire—Maribeth has discovered and reflects the path to prosperity. Real wealth is discovered in the heart and Maribeth Morrissey has a heart of gold. Thank you, Maribeth for being an abundant blessing to the world. I'm so grateful to know you!"

— Dr. Darren Weissman, Best Selling Author of *The Power of Infinite Love and Gratitude* and Developer of The LifeLine Technique®

"Aurora Farber's exemplary journey into prosperity through the discovery and rediscovery of her mythic feminine essence opens a doorway to one's own abundant reality. With a generosity of spirit she gives each reader seeds planted in thirty years of journal entries, intense reflection and the meaningful images that frame her narrative—symbols both ambrosial and palpable. These are sparks of the feminine fire forged with courage, lyricism and love."

—Kath O'Brien Wooddell, Porcupine Storytelling

"Nicole Hemmer points out common mis-perceptions around the topic of money. She clearly sees that especially in spiritual communities, people can block their impact by not embracing money as a divine tool to bring healing and raise the vibration on the planet. Nicole brings awareness to how important it is to change our mindset. Her chapter is a powerful piece that will boost your impact, power, and influence as a spiritual being in the world. She writes, 'Truly, the world is in need of spiritual billionaires, conscious beings using the tool of money for the restructuring of this Earth, one that's in sync with the heart and the Earth.' I recommend this book for anyone wishing to open their heart and mind to a different viewpoint on money."

— Jonas Meteling, Certified Coach and Creator of the Light-Healing Program

"It's as if Mia Luz channeled the energy of Mother Gaia in to every letter of every word. The alchemy of ink against paper is like the breath of our beloved Earth Mother, comforting our souls with a language found inside a language whispering—you are love, you are safe, you are perfect just as you are."

—Libby Piper

"Lainie Love's chapter is beautiful. Her beliefs are fierce and make me want to jump on the boat and fight for what's right and sacred and abundant!"

—S.S.

"As Maribeth's story of abundance illustrates, it is by moving through our life challenges that we discover the true gift of Self. Maribeth has beautifully found her way and now supports others to do the same. I have tremendous respect, and admiration for the path she has traveled, the wisdom she has gained and her desire to share it with others. Maribeth's rare compassionate heart provides a genuine path of healing, so that others may receive forgiveness and acceptance for themselves and their families."

—Peggy Rometo, Intuitive Expert, Author of *The Little Book of Big Promises*

FLOWER OF LIFE PRESS
Voices of Transformation

Cover and interior artwork by Lainie Love Dalby
Book design by Jane Ashley, floweroflifepress.com

To contact the publisher, visit
floweroflifepress.com

Library of Congress Control Number: 2018952259
Flower of Life Press, Old Saybrook, CT.

ISBN-13: 978-0986353963

Printed in the United States of America

Are You Ready To Be A Published Author?

Books are the best business card you can have, whether you are an entrepreneur building your company, or a changemaker with a message that needs to be heard. Flower of Life Press is committed to giving voice to authors—and offering the support that is critical to birthing an authentic and powerful book.

We are ready to serve you with writing coaching, editing, and design while we provide the marketing team that will propel your journey and electrify your audience!

Check us out now at **floweroflifepress.com**—and have your book published by the team with over 3,000 books to their credit!

DEDICATION

Dedicated to YOU, dear reader~
*May you open to love, embody compassion, speak
your truth with clarity, and gratefully receive the
infinite prosperity and abundance that is all around
you in each moment.*

Dedicated to my husband Scott Watrous~
*Thank you for showing up at the perfect time and
doing the work with me. Our love is the portal
into my Soul's evolution and I am so grateful to be on
this Path of Prosperity together.*

THE GREENING POWER OF THE GODDESS, 2018

Artist: Lainie Love Dalby
Medium: Mixed media shamanic healing he(art) collage

I believe in the power of art making itself as a form of prayer, deep healing, and communion with the Divine. It is a portal/vehicle for the secret language of the soul that helps lure us back to wholeness. That's why I refer to my Shamanic Healing artworks as He(art). It's accessing an endless well of colorful textured language from the mysterious realm of the Great Mystery and the depths of our heart and soul. Each sacred offering is a clue to the truth of who we are, leading us closer to ourselves and why we're here at this time. It's an opportunity for us to take an individual journey into our inner landscapes, bringing forth our deepest expression and the embodied truth felt deep in our bones. I innately know, sense and feel that every creation is inscribed with the mark of the Creator, including each and every one of us.

Because of this, I deeply believe that each and every one of us matters and that we're here to DO something that matters. We each have a precious human life that deserves to be cherished, supported and upheld as part of the larger web of ALL life. It's fundamental to the air I breathe and each step I take in the world. I operate from the basic premise that we're all artists in charge of the greatest masterpiece on earth, our LIVES. We all have a Divine Legacy that we're co-creating each day, all in service to the Great Cosmic Masterpiece. We must each add our unique stroke to this collective masterpiece, or else it will be forever lost.

Two of the ways I personally do this are through my embodied leadership mentoring and shamanic healing he(art)works focused on individual and social transformation. A core part of my medicine is bringing the visionary unseen realms into the seen here-and-now-reality, including with this commissioned he(art) work on the cover.

The Greening Power of the Goddess is a symbolic transmission of the Divine Feminine principles for regeneration and sustenance outlined in my chapter "Igniting a Sacred (R)evolution: a.k.a. A New Bottom Line of Love". As the title

hints, there is a Greening Power of the Goddess, to this FLOUR-ISHING that we so deeply desire, this restoration of reverence for all of life. It is root, infinity, earth, flowering, opening, blossoming, sweet nourishing honey dripping, womb, creation, vision, regeneration, juiciness, cosmic service, interconnection, spiral dance, Kundalini rising, transformation, creation, LIFE, death and rebirth of society.

I received this full image as a vision in a dream and brought it into reality for this commission. It was a direct inspiration and download from Spirit. The images that speak to me are universal, tapping into the nature of the cosmos and all that is, relating to our intimate connectedness with others and all of life, and reminding us of who we are and to whom we belong.

For many years I have had deep connection and communion with all the symbols included since they originate from my ancestral heritage and spiritual lineages: the ankh symbolizes eternal LIFE, the infinity sign/lemniscate symbolizes abundance and limitless supply, and the triple Goddess spiral in the center represents the life, death and rebirth mysteries. Additionally, the eagle and snake are two of my main spirit animals that have been journeying with me for most of my life and symbolize vision and transformation respectively.

Words can't do this he(art) work justice however. In truth there is a much greater richness to the image if you just sit with it and allow the Great Mystery to unfold before you as a guide to its deeper wisdom. May it be a blessing and a visual prayer that helps us to pioneer new pathways to prosperity.

Learn more about Lainie Love Dalby or commission your own Shamanic Healing He(art) work at **www.lainielovedalby.com** or on Instagram @ **LainieLoveDalby.**

CONTENTS

Introduction

BY JANE ASHLEY, *PUBLISHER*

My path to prosperity has been a wild ride! Now that this book is going to press, I can look back and truly see how I created this entire project so that I could take my own medicine and learn how to expand into the energy of prosperity. Working with twenty-five authors while editing, designing, and publishing this book has been an exercise into the rewiring of my own scarcity and lack consciousness! I am SO grateful for this experience—I've gone from someone who was afraid to look at the numbers in my checking account out of fear and extreme panic to someone who is rarely charged or triggered around money at all anymore. And it's because I now understand at a cellular level, that *abundance is an inside job.* And that I can create it in an instant and receive the blessings that the universe has in store for me.

When I made the decision to declare bankruptcy in 2017, I knew I was setting myself up for a huge initiation around receiving. It was time to stop avoiding money. Time to stop running from the chronic feeling of not enoughness. It was time to stop undercharging and undervaluing my services. It was time to begin to face myself and my unconscious patterning around money and lack of self-worth. It was time to change and evolve!

The wisdom in this collection of voices is incredible and priceless. The authors have gifted us their stories and practices so that anyone who is ready to face themselves and their shadow around money can do so in a container that is *real*. There is no bullshit coming your way in this book. I am living proof that this book really will transform you—if you let it.

Inside these pages, you'll find many gems—including these highlights:

Alexis Neely invites you to question if your relationship to money is causing you to compromise the truth of who you are in ways that you may not even be able to see. Once you get real, free yourself from the trap of money dysmorphia and come into right relationship with time, money and how you get paid, you'll be able to find true, everlasting, uncompromised prosperity.

In "Getting Off the Worry Wheel: How I Trust My Needs Will Be Met", Tanya Lynn Paluso shares the defining moment when she experienced a miracle that altered her relationship with money forever. Her words will inspire you to find a deeper level of TRUST so you are no longer stressed out, worried or anxious about money—no matter how much you have in your bank account.

Alis Mao shares her journey from the Killing Fields of Cambodia to the "land of promise"—the United States—and how her mother taught her the timeless wisdom that real prosperity and "the good life" requires a heart filled with love, forgiveness, compassion, and generosity without reservation.

Alokananda shares his journey of building what he calls "true prosperity"— the cutting edge of where purpose, service, deep fulfillment, financial freedom, and earth stewardship converge.

In "Igniting a Sacred (R)evolution", Lainie Love Dalby offers the medicine of reconnection for our ailing world as well as practical, grounded advice to help restore the sacred Feminine back into balance in our world so that we can make LOVE the bottom line once again.

Mia Luz's chapter will awaken your desire to reconnect with nature and our Earth, and bring a solidified awareness of abundance and prosperity to your life.

Cora Poage offers tangible internal and external strategies for Financial Freedom so you can feel free right here and right now, whatever your money situation might be.

Megan Luther offers a reflection of her inner experience of awakening and her process of redefining the concept of value. She shares daily practices to help develop feeling navigation and intuition, and to recognize the illusions that we create in our lives.

Inspired by the journals and journeys of her life, Aurora Farber invites you to partner with your "mythic essence" as a guide, so that you become a vessel for the abundance of delight, love, and possibility that is all around.

Amanda Leigh's chapter, "Facing Me" will inspire you to develop a more intimate and loving relationship with yourself, see your vulnerabilities as strengths, and open up to receive far more love, abundance, and prosperity than you can even imagine!

Nicole Hemmer shares a sacred invocation for the reclamation of money as a powerful tool and conduit for love, beauty, and transformation in the world, as well as the remembrance that we are one with the energy of money and that abundance is our divine birthright.

With ritual burials, blind privilege, and tiny miracles, Alexandra Pallas invites you "Into the Arms of Abundance"—a poetic expression of the many faces of the goddess-muse Abundantia, and a vulnerable exploration of the interplay of abandonment, spiritual debt, entitlement, gratitude, and magic—highlighting what happens when we take a hard look at what our relationship with prosperity is asking of us.

Gavin Pauley offers a new perspective on human interaction, sexuality and gender, with suggestions for staying in the flow of abundance and prosperity.

In "Re-Storying Our Economy," Samantha Sweetwater challenges our assumptions and gives us a far reaching yet practical new framework for how to move our money and our abundant life into the New Paradigm of personal and collective thriving.

In "Flowing in the Stream of Grace and Abundance," Allison Conte offers timely prosperity practices to enhance and elevate your wealth consciousness so that you can deepen into trust, gratitude and Divine Love. She also shares important lessons about the misuse of power and the incredible freedom that comes with forgiveness.

Kate Mulder offers insight into why your intuition and full spectrum intelligence is your most powerful business asset—and guides you to receive the most aligned potential in your business endeavors. Additionally, Kate provides a higher perspective on the rapid paradigm shift that is currently happening in our global economy, and how to best prepare, prosper, and thrive through this transition.

I applaud you for picking up this book and saying YES to your unique journey to prosperity. Read it and just witness the miracles as your vibration shifts and abundance shows up for you!

May your journey on the Path of Prosperity be one of liberation—and the ride of a lifetime!

Jane Ashley, MA, CHHC is the embodiment of every fractal of her journey. As Mom, wife, and daughter, she navigates this dimension—holding space for love and empathy.

As the Publisher of her company, Flower of Life Press, she creates books and brands as sacred containers of essence and change for her community. Jane fearlessly brings forward those urgent and poignant conversations necessary as we navigate these fractious times in our world.

As a leader in the rising feminine movement, Jane understands the importance of collaboration and community in the new economy. Her background as a psychotherapist, book designer, branding consultant, and visionary has brought Jane a deep knowing of her purpose on the planet.

Her latest book series, *The New Feminine Evolutionary,* catalyzes our collective evolution, providing personal stories, wisdom, and active tools to obliterate blocks, uncover truths, and support All of Life.

Like single sticks piled together, Jane's work and life have become one energy—fueling a sacred fire circle surrounded by kindred souls—a celebration of life and the voices that are lighting the path for all of us to follow. On this path, you'll discover books that matter, a community that thrives together, and the freedom to speak truth without judgment.

Connect with Jane at **floweroflifepress.com**.

Your Personal Money Map to Prosperity: Free Yourself from the Trap of Money Dysmorphia

BY ALEXIS NEELY

CHASING PROSPERITY

For years, I chased prosperity—and got it. Kind of. At least from the outside, it appeared that way.

I built two million-dollar companies, wrote a best-selling book, was appearing regularly on television, had a house a half a block from the beach, sent the kids in private school...the whole nine.

By anyone's standards, I had made it.

I should have felt prosperous and abundant, but I didn't.

I had a great business and the ability to make all the money I could have possibly needed, and yet I was emotionally and spiritually bankrupt.

You see, I couldn't appreciate what I had created. Instead, it all felt like a huge burden. I was terrified most of the time, questioning myself constantly, and horribly uncertain about whether I was making the right decisions.

"Am I doing enough?"

"Will I be able to keep this going?"

"Does s/he only like me because of my money or what s/he thinks I can do for him/her?"

"Am I on the right path?" "Do I even like the work I am doing or am I only doing it for the money?"

"Is the work I've created even valuable in the world, or am I just a really good saleswoman?"

"What should I be spending my time on?"

"Is this a good use of my resources?"

"Should I make that investment?"

"Is s/he trying to take advantage of me?"

"Am I getting my money's worth here?"

Although I had plenty of money, I did not have true prosperity. I knew there was something else possible: a feeling of ease around money, a knowing I had enough, a certainty that I was doing the work I was meant to do, in the way I was meant to do it, and that I was being paid properly for that work. That would feel like true prosperity to me, if only I could figure out how to have it.

FALSE CORE BELIEFS

All the incessant questioning, and my reactions and behaviors that arose from that questioning, stemmed from a core belief I carried with me from childhood. This core belief led me to make consistently poor decisions about how I used my Time, my Energy, my Attention, and my Money (I call these TEAM resources). Due to this core belief, I hurt relationships that will never recover. I made investments that reinforced my belief that I couldn't handle what I was creating. And I used my money to try to buy myself security and assurance that I would be loved.

The truth is, I didn't really know how to have relationships because the only thing I really thought about when it came to relationships was how much the relationship would cost me or how much it would make me.

I had no clear vetting process for investments and was usually too afraid to ask the hard questions that would reveal what was true because I didn't want to be disliked.

The saying "money can't buy you love" is an absolute truth. My emotional and spiritual bankruptcy would ultimately lead me to financial bankruptcy, where I was able to discover the truth of prosperity and what it takes to really have it.

At the bottom of the bottom, I got to see the truth of who I was, and I didn't like her.

As Sara Blakely, the founder of the billion-dollar company Spanx, is quoted as saying: *"I feel like money makes you more of who you already are. If you're an asshole, you become a bigger asshole."*

That was definitely the truth for me.

While I considered myself someone who cared about people, that caring was mostly trapped beneath a dis-ease of epic proportions that nearly ruined my life and most certainly didn't make the lives of the people around me very pleasant either.

In so many ways, I was an asshole. The scary part about it, though, is that I was blind to it, due to a common disease that I believe most of us have. And, it's a disease that's extremely difficult to see or diagnose because it's so common in our culture.

THE FIRST SIGNS OF DIS-EASE

In fact, you just might have this disease yourself. If you do, it really doesn't matter how much money you make, it will never be enough. If you have this disease, you'll never feel prosperous or abundant. If you have this disease, you are probably an asshole too, and may not even know it.

Instead, what you will likely do (and are probably doing right now) is compromise your life, your time, your energy, your attention, and your relationships. And maybe even blame others for that compromise.

The worst part is, you won't even know it's happening, though you will be aware that something isn't right because no matter how much money you make, it will never be enough.

It's not your fault though, really. It's the disease. It's blinding because it makes you think you don't have what you need and that you must compromise because if you don't you'll starve, or be homeless, or never be able to support yourself, or not be good enough, or never prove it to them, or...well, you know the stories, I am sure, because you've got your own personal version of them, probably secretly motivating you, possibly in ways you can't even see.

Prosperity Exercise

Get out your journal and write out your biggest fear when it comes to money and what will happen to you if you don't have enough of it, or if you run out of what you do have. Let's surface the truth of what's motivating you here so you can begin to spot where the fear of "not enough" is running your life.

As a result of this disease, you have thoroughly convinced yourself you have to work that job you hate, or stay in that marriage or relationship you can't stand, or go to that event you really don't want to go to, or be friends with that person you would rather just not, or invest in that company that you know is hurting the planet, or buy that disposable thing because you can't afford the one that's more expensive, but won't end up in the landfill, or not do that thing you really want to do, and you just know would change your life...because, well, you don't have enough money to make a different choice.

Do you see what I'm saying here?

You long for prosperity and abundance, and yet every choice you make is based on a diseased reality, *a distorted view*.

WHERE ARE YOU BLINDLY COMPROMISING DUE TO DIS-EASED UNDERSTANDING OF MONEY?

How much would you need to have before you stopped compromising? Or before you got truly generous, as you claim you want to be?

It doesn't matter. Because if you are compromising now, or not being generous now, there's no amount of money that will ever be enough—not until you see the disease that has been running your life, wake up from it, and start making your choices with your eyes wide open, clear, sober, awake, and aware.

When you begin making your choices with your eyes wide open, you can relate to money, and compromise, and generosity, and the life you really want, from a place of health.

What will it take for you to get there?

Will it be a forced financial crisis? Or a health crisis? A spiritual crisis? A business crisis? A marriage crisis?

Will you be willing to see what's true before it takes everything you have from you and you are forced to rebuild from the bottom of the bottom, like I did?

Ultimately, this is your choice. If you are on a the path to true prosperity, you will either be forced to discover what's true or you will choose to excavate the truth, consciously.

The path of true prosperity will require you to grow up and see what's actually true, one way or another.

Prosperity Exercise
What's the truth about where you are compromising for or because of money? Get out your journal and write out all the places and ways you compromise. Is it in your work? Is it in your giving? Is it in one or more relationships? Acknowledge now, in the privacy of your own journey, where you are not being who you want to be because of (or for) money.

FORCE OR CHOICE?

For me to see what was true, I had to be forced. I simply could not make the choices that were necessary for me to face reality.

Instead, I had to hit absolute rock bottom, "forced" to move from a 3,800-square-foot house into a two-bedroom ramshackle farmhouse, "forced" to give up all of my "help," and "forced" to let go of everything I thought I was creating, so I could watch my life unravel.

As it was happening, I was often torn between surrender grasping in terror as I tried to hold on.

In 2010, after moving to Colorado because I knew I had to get out of the ego-inducing Los Angeles and the gossip TV shows I was appearing on as a legal expert, I spent every day crying on the phone to the interim CEO I had hired to run my company because I knew I couldn't keep it all together alone.

Everyday, as I cried, he asked me, "Lex, what do you want?" Each day, I whined back to him "Hitch, I don't knoooowwwwwww."

I thought I had wanted what I had created. But then I felt trapped by it. And burdened. And from that place, I was an asshole. Because I thought I needed to be. And because I thought I was entitled to be. I mean, I was doing all the work to support everyone, right? Oy.

Hitch proceeded to decrease my overhead by more than half by firing pretty much everyone who worked for me or by setting such clear boundaries that they quit. I had never really learned to set boundaries clearly, so when Hitch came in and started doing so, it really shook things up. I had been overpaying some people to deal with my guilt about how difficult I was to work with. And, I was underpaying others, probably crossing their boundaries without any sensitivity to their needs because I was so focused on meeting my own. Hitch cut back the overhead with the hopes of buying

5

me back the space to discover what I really wanted, bringing it down. He cut the overhead to a manageable level I could actually handle.

As Hitch cut everything back, I got more and more terrified. While I felt burdened by my high overhead and generally unappreciative of all the people supporting me because I couldn't tell who was supporting me and who was taking from me, I also felt terrified that if I didn't have the support I couldn't make money. And, underlying it all, if I didn't have money, I wouldn't have any love.

Hitch disabused me of that notion one day in August 2011, when he suggested I face my biggest fear and let myself run out of money, completely. "Just do it," he said.

"But, I won't be able to pay my bills, including paying you," I said. "Everyone will hate me."

"It's okay, Lex. Everyone loves you. At least the people who matter. Let it go. See what's there for you."

HOW I WAS FORCED (SUPPORTED) TO SEE THE TRUTH

I never would have been able to see the truth if I had not come across two additional timely and pointed resources to help me see where I was actually off the path.

The first was Lynne Twist's book "The Soul of Money" and her teachings around sufficiency. Lynne says that sufficiency isn't about cutting back or lowering expectations. "Sufficiency," she says, "is a context we bring forth from within that reminds us that if we look around us and within ourselves, we will find what we need. There is always enough."

I loved these ideas, and yet didn't know how to actually find them inside myself. They were beautiful words with no actual meaning inside of me. I was still sure I needed millions of dollars accumulated in my bank and retirement accounts to be free.

Then I met the $100 million man and saw clearly how very wrong I was, and I got a very clear view of the trap I was creating for myself.

I knew he was a $100 million man because it's all he could talk about: where the money was, what form it was in, how he could access it. At the same time, he was still working harder in his business than anyone else I had met. Not because he needed to for the money, but because he didn't seem to have anything better to do.

The $100 million man's relationships were painfully shallow, his fear prominent, and his primary security came from the gold and silver and bills and coins he had piled in various places across the planet. He was more trapped than anyone I had ever met, living in excess (in stark contrast to sufficiency) and yet still seeking more.

Meeting him, and reading Lynne's book, and with Hitch's encouragement, I saw that I would need to face the truth that everything I had created was from a place of "not enoughness" and it was time to find my own sufficiency, rooted and grounded in reality, on my path to true prosperity.

So I did. I faced my biggest fears. I let it all go. I did the thing I said I never would, and moved to the farm with my kids.

And for the first time in my adult life, I was no longer the breadwinner. I was no longer the one who paid people to do things for me. I was stripped bare.

Stripped Bare.

I grocery shopped, and cooked, and drove my kids around. And felt certain I had failed with no hope of ever returning to this thing I had called success and prosperity.

What I discovered in that year was that there was a far greater possibility of success and prosperity available to me when I remembered who I was, why I was here and what was really mine to do.

Because, until I was choosing to live from the truth of my being, I would never feel fulfilled, no matter how much "success and prosperity" I created.

And the first thing I would need in order to live from truth, and remember who I was, why I was here, and what was mine to do would be to get into right relationship with time, money, and how I got paid.

Doing that made me face that I had been living with a painful disease. A disease that had kept me blind. A disease that keeps many of us blind. A disease that has most of us compromising what really matters to us and creating a world that doesn't really work for anyone.

My hope is though that I did the work for many of us, and that if you are reading this now it's because you are ready to wake up, see the disease that's driving you and make a different choice without having to lose everything to do it.

So, what is this disease?

MONEY DYSMORPHIA, REVEALED.

It's called *money dysmorphia*. And it's the distorted view that most of us have about money that causes us to make poor decisions about, well, everything. But, mostly it causes us to make poor decisions about how we use our non-renewable assets: our time, our energy and our attention.

And the really sad part of this is that money is infinitely renewable. You can always, always, always make more money. But once you've given up your time, your energy, and your attention, it's gone forever.

The good news is that once you see your money dysmorphia, you can begin to awaken to right relationship with time, money, and how you get paid, in a way that will bring you all the prosperity you want and need. And you'll stop compromising. I imagine you'll also be generous in all the best ways, supporting a world that truly works for everyone. And that's the path to true, everlasting, prosperity. Not just for you, but for all of us.

But first, it takes seeing the money dysmorphia. Once you see it, you can make your life choices based on clarity and truth.

So, how do you see it?

GETTING TO THE TRUTH OF WHAT YOU REALLY, REALLY, REALLY, REALLY WANT

Seeing your money dysmorphia, and on the flip side, your path to prosperity, requires you to get honest with yourself, first and foremost, about the life you really, really, really, REALLY want. Getting honest with yourself often requires digging deeper than the surface beliefs about what you think you want.

For example, on the surface you may think you are totally fine just getting by. You've gotten so used to not having much that you have resigned yourself to the belief that just getting by is all that's possible. Or you don't let yourself dare to dream of more than just getting by because you may be disappointed if that's all you can have. You may even tell yourself that your desires for more aren't "spiritual" or that if you have more someone else has to have less.

If any of that is the case, note it. Begin to consider where those beliefs came from, and if they are serving you. Most likely they are roadblocks on your path to prosperity because they aren't what's true. What's true is that there is more than enough for everyone. You having more actually makes it more likely that others around you can have more too.

Or perhaps you're focused on living the big life. You've got a million-dollar business. You're drawn in by every Internet marketing ad out there promising you that you can make it big while working less.

You can have the "big life," but first you need to get honest about where you are now and then map the path from here to there.

But, if you already have enough, you need to look at what you really need to have the life you want. Think about whether you are chasing the big life to distract yourself from the thing you really want, that you think maybe you can't have.

Just getting by, chasing the big life, or somewhere in between...it all starts with getting honest about what you really, really, really, REALLY want.

I recommend you do this at four different levels of reality.

1. Minimum to be happy.
2. Minimum to be of service.
3. Preferred, if you could afford it.
4. No limits.

Describe your life at each of these four levels, in as much detail as you can. Where do you live? What do you eat? Where do you travel? How do you exercise? I have a program that takes you through thirty different categories to consider. You can find a link to it in my bio at the end of this chapter.

It's important to look at each of these levels, no matter where you are now, because your truth exists on a spectrum. What you really, really, really, REALLY want isn't a single, static thing. You are an ever-changing, evolutionary being. And you may just find that when you have all of your needs met and you are doing work you love that perhaps a more minimal life meets you fully.

Or, you may find that your dreams are so big, and your visions so clear, that you actually need a $1M (or even a $10M) company.

Once you've mapped out each of the levels, you can get honest about where you are now in relation to each of those levels.

Are you living a life that is below your minimum to be happy? Or maybe you've already got enough money to be living your preferred if you could afford it, and it's time to stop thinking incessantly about saving more money and instead start thinking about how you can use money to buy back your time.

Once you are honest about the life and income you really, really, really, REALLY want (on all four levels) and where you are now, you can chart a path from exactly where you are now to where you want to go next.

This is the key to your path to prosperity. Seeing through the money dysmorphia. Getting real with what you need, what you already have, and how to use your TEAM resources in service to the truth.

When you know what you need, and you know what you have, and you can ask for what you need in exchange for what you have, you can never not have enough. It does require you to know what you need, which many of us don't because of money dysmorphia. And it does require you to know what you have, which also many of us don't because of money dysmorphia. And it does require to know how to ask, which many of us don't because we never learned.

But, it's time you do. Because this is your path to true prosperity.

REMEMBERING WHO YOU ARE, WHY YOU ARE HERE, AND WHAT'S YOURS TO DO

When I came to see my money dysmorphia and got into right relationship with time, money, and how I get paid, I was able to remember who I am, why I am here, and what's mine to do.

It's not an overnight process. In fact, for me, it took seven years of spiraling around and around the wheel, sometimes going all the way back down after I was already on an upswing. Partially, that's because I had to invent the process I've shared with you here, and I didn't have anyone who could see me clearly and direct me to open my eyes and make better choices.

The good news though is that each time I spiraled and returned to this process of clarity that I've shared with you here, more was revealed. And I never again had to let go of everything like I did in 2011. Instead, I've been able to let go of only that which needed to be released to make space for what was more in alignment.

Today I am living in true prosperity. My company that trains lawyers earned $2.4 million in revenue last year (our biggest year yet), and we've got a fantastic team of twenty. I no longer make decisions that compromise my truth, my generosity, or my integrity.

Best of all, I know exactly what I need, how to ask for and receive it gracefully, and how to give what I have generously (and not as a secretly disguised attempt to get something), and I remember who I am, why I'm here, what's mine to do. To me, this is what makes life worth living.

Alexis Neely (artist name: Ali Shanti) is a bridge between the generations. She graduated first in her law school class from Georgetown and today uses her law degree to uplevel the con-sciousness of the legal field, and the families and business owners served by lawyers. Ali serves as a catalyst for new ways of thinking, a paradigm-shifter, lawyer, mom, author, and permission giver who is bringing forward radically new and much needed perspectives on how we make decisions about money, time, work, relationships, parenting and business. And she offers her personal experiences with living a new paradigm, road less traveled life to serve as a model of what's possible when we allow all of ourselves to show up fully in family, life and business.

Special Gift

Dive into the Money Map to Freedom process yourself, for free, at **www.eyeswideopenlife.com** and get started creating your own Money Map there.

Getting Off the Worry Wheel: How I Trust My Needs Will Be Met

BY TANYA LYNN PALUSO

My credit cards maxed. Negative balance in my bank account. Mounting debt. Last week I reluctantly asked my mom for gas money. I'm scrambling to figure out how I would pay my $575 rent.

How on earth could I do a book launch next weekend without enough money to purchase books to sell?

I felt that old tightening feeling in my stomach, knots of tension and anxiety. For the past nine months, I had been deep in a healing process, systematically going through each area of my life and the limited beliefs that held me back from my full potential.

This, my relationship with money, was the last on the list. The area I kept avoiding...until I couldn't look away any longer. Here it was, the biggest obstacle preventing me from my big dream as a published author.

I needed a solution. Fast.

I couldn't think straight. But I knew what to do...the thing I had been doing every morning for the past four months: go out to the trail to release and pray.

I put on my yoga pants and tank top, laced up my running shoes, grabbed a jacket and headed down the street to the end of the road where the trail to the lagoon starts. At 8 a.m. in March in North Coastal San Diego, the air felt cool and crisp, perfect temperature for a morning workout.

Except this wasn't your typical workout; this was deep somatic release work.

As I passed over the gate onto the dirt trail, a memory surfaced in my mind. I was brushing my hair in my bathroom at twelve years old, and my dad came in and stood there crying. Stunned, I just looked at him, unsure what to say. He told me that his business, a million-dollar dentistry practice, was in a slow period. Stressed, worried, and hard on himself, he wanted to let me know that things may get tight. We lived in a huge house and I always got what I wanted, never mind what I needed. Money never felt like a concern. It was always just there.

This conversation confused me. While things never changed and I still always got what I wanted, the memory continued to stick with me and the beliefs haunted me for years to come.

"No matter how hard you work, you'll always stress about money."

"Don't trust money will always be there."

"There is never enough money."

"Running a business is hard work and you'll struggle."

More than twenty years later, I came face to face with these beliefs, unable to run from them anymore. They sabotaged me, keeping me a slave to my business, working harder to create more and more value while I still barely had enough money to live.

Like Arjuna going to war in the *Bhagavad Gita*, I had to go to war against this gang of subconscious beliefs and release myself once and for all from their death grip. As an illusion of my mind's eye, it was up to me to fight them to their death. Seeing the impact and how they had wreaked havoc on my life, I was ready. Systematically, I jogged up and down the hill, symbolically hitting limiting beliefs with my elbows, leaving them behind me as I climbed the summit toward my freedom, crying as I told each one that I was done. "NO MORE!" I screamed. "NO MORE NO MORE NO MORE!"

After the final one, panting and crying toward the bottom of the hill, I fell to the ground onto my knees and looked up at the sky. "God!" I cried. "I've got this book launch next weekend and I need $1,000 by tonight. Midnight. You got that God?! You've got a deadline. If you really want me to put this book out there in the world, if it's really meant to be, then show me the money. Tell me what to do. I will do anything. Just tell me."

I stopped and held my breath, listening. Then I heard it, softly.

"Tell them the truth."

Oh God...really?!

I knew exactly what that meant. I marched back up the hill to the house. I had two calls scheduled that morning with Laura Hollick and Christina Dunbar. As I shared with each of them, they both gave me great advice that I probably would not have taken to heart in the past. Then I called my editor who suggested asking friends to pre-order the book so I had some money up front. And finally, I called my best friend who told me she'd loan me some money.

Feeling more confident after reaching out for support, I knew I could no longer procrastinate on the thing I knew I needed to do.

Tell them the truth.

I opened up my computer, took a deep breath and began to type.

Tell them the truth.

My friends like Anat, Laura, and Christina would accept me no matter what. But what would everyone else think? How could I put a book about leadership out there if I was broke? The shame rose up in my body, causing me to choke up. Hot tears stung my eyes.

This felt a million times more vulnerable than a couple years ago when I told my parents about my $17,000 debt, which was the hardest conversation I had ever had.

Now to cast a spotlight on my shadow—the irresponsible fraud—for my whole world to see?

My stomach did a somersault. I cleared my mind and started to write. I read it twice before I finally mustered up the courage to hit Send to my email list at 3:37 p.m. and then hit post on Facebook. Here's what I wrote:

Dear friend,

If you are an entrepreneur, you know what it is like to keep investing into your business or a big project.

That's where I'm at and I've completely hit an edge.

I need to order the books by Wednesday for the San Diego launch party and I've got nothing left. Every dime has gone into self-publishing this book. Credit is maxed. I've actually never been at this place before so it feels extremely vulnerable.

I've been crying off and on all day. A million limited beliefs have been running through my head.

You are a fraud.
You aren't worthy.
You are a failure.
Give up.
Quit.

The list goes on...
I had three important conversations in the past twenty-four hours that have helped me come back into alignment.

CONVERSATION #1 WITH LEELA: OPEN YOUR HEART TO RECEIVE.

Last night, I had dinner with my dear friend Leela Somaya and as I shared the process I've been going through, she said something like: 'It sounds like you are not opening your heart to receive all that is all around you."

Sometimes, what you need is right in front of your face; you are just too stuck in your head to see it.

CONVERSATION #2 WITH LAURA: YOU ARE EXPANDING YOUR CAPACITY.

This morning, I had a collaboration call with Laura Hollick, who said that artists normally don't allow themselves the opportunity to expand their capacity right before a big launch. That's why I'm experiencing this pain and discomfort...I am literally stretching myself to be able to hold the energy that could potentially come my way with my book launch.

Laura shared the story about her first International Soul Art Day with 15,000 people showing up, which knocked her down afterward. She wasn't "ready" for that energy to be hurling toward her...and now I have an opportunity to prepare myself and be ready for it, by the grace of God giving me some big obstacles and all my shit coming up around it.

CONVERSATION #3 WITH CHRISTINA: YOU ARE THE EMBODI-MENT OF YOUR WORK.

After I interviewed Christina Dunbar on Google Hangout today, she held space for me to fall apart. How can I embody my work? What is my edge of vulnerability? Well, of course, going public with my process. Asking for support. "But I don't wanna!" my little voice whined.

Yet here I am. And that's what makes me powerful in the world. I don't let an empty bank account stop me. I'm not going to buy into the story that money = self-worth. Because money doesn't make me who I am.

We always have a choice:

Be stopped by your circumstance and fail to see the lesson, or see the grace of God in the circumstance, flow with it, and grow from it.

I will not be stopped. So I started sharing today. I started asking for support.

My best friend showed up big time. She told me that she's been here before and now she's got money in the bank, which she wants to use to support the people in her life, so she'd be happy to lend me the money to order the books. I have been crying in gratitude because this is the second time a dear friend has shown up for me when I was on my knees needing support. The other time was in 2011 when my boyfriend broke up with me and one of my best friends opened her home up for me to heal.

I have so much gratitude for being able to see clearly what God wants me to see. This is all part of my healing: Can I open my heart to receive the love and support all around me?

Yes.

And so I will embody the work and open my heart even wider and ask for your support.

My mind tried to trick me and say, well, you don't have to share the full vulnerable story since you're covered for Wednesday. But then I wouldn't actually be getting the message fully: Share from the most vulnerable, authentic place. Be with this—all of it. The details of your story matter. You matter.

I need $868.88 to order the books. Here's how you can help (and it is ALWAYS a win-win in my world):

** If you live in San Diego:

==>> Pre-order your paperback today here.

I'm only going to have a limited amount of books for sale at the book launch party so this guarantees you will get one! It's $15 (list price is $19.95) pre-order...pick it up, signed by me, at the book launch party on March 22. If you can't make it to the party, you can stop by my house for pick up after March 20.

** If you live somewhere else:

==>> Pay-what-you-can for an hour coaching with me.

If you are someone who is stopped by your circumstances, this is the opportunity to break through. This is my genius. I make it happen and I help others make it happen. I help people get out of their heads and see the truth of who they are. I empower you to see your worth and get freed up from the stories and limited beliefs that you've bought into from your lineage.

Not clear on what's holding you back? Not sure on what's blocking you? That's what I'm here to help you identify and then move through. No more denial. No more avoiding. Let's face the truth together so you've got someone in your corner, supporting you, rooting you on, as you break through.

Most importantly, I've discovered how to balance self-effort with the grace of God so your action is not burning you out. The integration of masculine and feminine, womb and heart, mind and spirit.

An hour with me and you'll leave transformed and inspired. And if you are really game, I'll get you to take action right then on the phone with me. Why wait when we can produce results right there in the moment? There can be some major ROI on that hour if you get super intentional. That's what I'm here for: to serve.

Now you may be at the end of this page and ready to click away...please pause for a moment.

What if taking this one action opened your heart?

What if this book or this hour with me was the thing that shifted everything for you?

How much would that be worth to you?

That's how I look at this...you are reading this for a reason and you have a choice in this moment to say YES to what the universe has dropped right in your lap. What I have learned through all this is that everything is being given to us, we simply have to open and receive it.

My ears are perked up, I am paying attention and I am saying YES to everything that is showing up in my life right now. If someone offers me some-

*thing, I say YES despite any resistance because I know that God has my back
and is giving me exactly what I need...it's up to me to open my heart to receive.*

*Take a moment to receive from me. While this may seem like it is about
me and my book, this is really about you. God is using me as an opportunity
for you to receive what you need. Expand. Open. Say YES:*

==>> Pre-order your paperback today here .
==>> Pay-what-you-can for an hour coaching with me.

Love with all my heart,
Tanya

I slammed my laptop shut. Oh my God, I did it. Oh my God, what are they
going to think? The vulnerability hangover set in and I went outside.

Then my phone started blowing up. Text messages from friends asking
how else to support...could they share my post?

I opened up Facebook, seeing comment after comment of love.

Fifteen minutes later, I slowly opened up my laptop and with one eye
shut, I cautiously opened up my inbox.

You've got money! PayPal announced.

The money started pouring in.

At midnight on March 10, 2015, I totaled up all the money I had received
from my GREAT BIG ASK as I called it: $1,041. Individuals had donated
anywhere from $10 to $200.

Your wish is my command, God said. And I'll throw in a few extra dollars so you know I've got your back.

That's the power of telling the truth.

This experience profoundly shifted my relationship with money. I
learned that money was readily available to those who opened themselves to
receive. Money, ultimately, is an expression of love. Everyone who donated
did so because they loved me and wanted to support me.

All I needed to do was ask.

From that moment forward, I never worried about money again.

When my husband and I found out we were pregnant and moved in
together and found a home that cost more than we thought we could afford,
I trusted. We never missed a rent payment.

When I put everything into my three-day event Feminine Uprising Live and maxed out our credit cards, I trusted. I more than quadrupled that investment.

Even when that obscure conversation took place and I bought into the lies my dad told himself about working hard and worrying about money, deep down, a part of me knew that I would always be provided for.

As I am writing this chapter less than three months after giving birth and our monthly income has been half of what it was the month before, I am trusting.

I am trusting that the universe will always provide what I need.

Tanya Lynn Paluso is a "strategic activator"—gifted at coaching women to soar to new heights by putting together a plan that maximizes their talents and strengths and taking bold, courageous actions to fulfill on their intentions. Tanya is the visionary CEO behind the international organization, Sistership Circle, a worldwide sisterhood movement empowering women to step into their true  beauty, brilliance and boldness as feminine leaders. She started training facilitators to use her proven 12-week Circle Program based on her bestselling book *Open Your Heart: How to be a New Generation Feminine Leader*. She is also the author of *How to Lead Circle and a contributing author of The New Feminine Evolutionary: Embody Presence—Become the Change.*

She is a respected leader in the industry from clients and colleagues alike because she's the real deal, living and breathing her work.

She believes that the new model of feminine leadership is not about hierarchies of power but about circles of collaboration. For us to become true leaders, we must embrace our sisters as our allies and give one another permission to shine. Learn more at **sistershipcircle.com.**

Special Gift

Ready to increase your effectiveness as a transformational group facilitator? Sistership Circle has developed a proven system to have women engaged, connected and wanting more. Visit **sistershipcircle. com/ebook** to receive your FREE eBook *"How to Lead Circle"* where you'll discover 7 secrets to get women raving about your circle.

Dreaming Big In A World with Infinite Possibilities

BY ALIS MAO

What is prosperity?

According to the dictionary, Prosperity is defined as a successful, flourishing, or thriving condition, especially in financial respects; good fortune. The state of being prosperous.

So, if we are meant to be successful, flourish, and thrive financially, how much do we really need to sacrifice to get there? How do we know when we are living "the good life?" Does "the good life" enslave our souls so we become like robots? Do we need to hide our emotions, feelings, thoughts, and heart spark inside a deep dark cave, never to resurface, hoping that one day at retirement it will spring back up and we'll be able to bloom into the full fruition of life's abundance?

My soul weeps deeply at this thought. Why do we, as people, allow this to be the core of our heart and being? I have always been full of curiosity and my heart yearns to explore the sacred stories of the world, envisioning our potential as more expansive than we allow ourselves to be.

The death of my father and my mother's journey of escaping the killing fields of Cambodia and arriving in the United States with me and my brother have taught me how to live my life from the perspective of what *could* be rather than what *should* be. I have learned that there is a world of infinite possibilities available to me if I just allow myself to explore and not fear failure or the loss of what I have—whether material possessions, status quo, or reputation.

Growing up, my mother endured many hardships. (You can read full details in my upcoming book *The Garden of Hope*). She ruffled every feather along her path as a twenty-five year old woman with two small children, figuring out her next steps while trying to protect us and keep us safe. She struggled and sacrificed to make her way from Cambodia to an unknown and foreign place so we could live in the "promised land" where dreams come true...the land of the free. The United States of America.

Yes, we made it.

We became free from the Cambodian Civil War, the "Killing Fields," and free from having to run from murderers who took the lives of millions. But, our newfound freedom came with a whole new set of challenges as we searched for those infinite possibilities. My mother faced language barriers and had to begin at the bottom and accept any job she could. As a single young mother in an unfamiliar place a world away from her home, she had to make it work. She was in survival mode most of the time and prayed for the good fortune she had learned was possible from her Cambodian culture—good health, blessings, longevity, and prosperity.

Prosperity.

My mother sacrificed so much in order to provide "the good life" for us. I remember her dreaming of not having to work so hard and joking about one day having enough money and the time for a vacation to just relax. In all her years, she took one vacation. She devoted her life to working and creating abundance and prosperity. She never complained, and always reminded us to give with all of our hearts. Through my mother, I fostered a generous heart.

She would tell me that to be prosperous, my heart has to be filled with love, forgiveness, compassion, and generosity without reservation. Only then can we feel abundance. Only then can we cast fear aside and know we are always blessed and guided. Only then can we know that we are enough and have enough. Only then can we say we have "the good life." Nothing more, nothing less. But always just enough.

As I allow those last words to forever ring in my heart, "Nothing more, nothing less. But always just enough," I am aware that my own life has mimicked my mother's—as a single mother, sacrificing my own dreams to care and provide "the good life" for my two sons.

As I sit and dream out loud just as I had once done with my mother, I can't help but think of the *what ifs* of my own life. Through hard work, I have established a comfortable life for me and my children. They have grown up and are now young adults. My oldest is about to spread his wings and fly, venturing off on his own life's journey. They have grown up witnessing me working hard and getting through all of life's initiations—just as I had witnessed my own mother. They have also grown to know, appreciate and value all the blessings and hardships we have been gifted in this life. I am blessed with the job I have and the people I work with who teach me to be a better version of myself. I choose to see the light and lessons in each and every soul that God connects me with. Even as a woman in a male-dominated workplace, I am gifted many opportunities to endure and learn the lessons I am here to learn, while treasuring every bit of it.

At times, I become lost in my own daydreams of this big, vast world and the infinite opportunities available. And sometimes fear sets in and I can't help but be brought back to the reality of my responsibilities as a mother, as a fiancé to an amazing man, as an employee, as a tax-paying citizen, and as a human being here on earth trying to survive. My curiosity still travels and dreams endlessly. How can we balance our responsibilities and at the same time live the good life filled with security and prosperity?

My mother is now retired at the age of sixty-five. Not retired by choice, but because of the physical pain she is in from all her years of hard work. I see it as a dear blessing, because she will finally be able to take that vacation she has dreamed of and return to her hometown for a visit. She'll be able to reflect back on where she spent her childhood and earlier years, and see it in a new light. She'll be able to forgive those who had taken everything from her so she can finally live and feel the "good" and "prosperous" life.

My mother once said to me in Khmer, "Daughter, never let anyone take your dream away from your heart and soul. As long as you are able to do this, life will be good each and every day. This world and universe we live in does hold infinite possibilities. Whether we go out there and journey to awaken our souls or just let our minds travel and dream, either way, our soul awakens and prospers deeply. That, my daughter, is enough."

She is a wise woman, my mother. So I ask you to contemplate these questions: "How much is *enough* for you to live in prosperity? How much are you willing to sacrifice to *get there?* If you stop for a second and take a breath, you will find your feet are already on the path to prosperity and that it *is* all around you, ripe for the picking.

I pray for each and every one of you to discover your own sense of "prosperity" and to live a beautiful life filled with love, light, and abundance. You deserve all the blessings and richness from this world, galaxy, universe we live in.

You, alone, are enough. Keep dreaming.

Alis Mao, a featured author in *Pioneering the Path to Prosperity,* is a spiritual and energy healer, author, mother, lover of love, compassion, nature, and all of life's simple beauty, a giver, and a truth seeker. Her upcoming memoir *Garden of Hope: My Journey from the Killing Fields of Cambodia To a Life of Unconditional Love, Forgiveness, Compassion, and Trust* will be released in 2019. Alis lives in Oregon with her two sons.

Special Gift

Receive and see more deeply into your TRUTH with a
FREE Spiritual and Energy Healing Session with Alis.
Contact Alis at **life4kids@yahoo.com** to schedule your session.

Money and Earth Stewardship

BY ALOKANANDA

I was at a fork in the road, and I chose to go all in.

Whether you believe in destiny, free will, or fate, you have choices. We all do. And I made a choice to go all in.

I've made this choice at varying crossroads in my life, and it is always a process of deepening my commitment to letting something greater than myself take over. This, from my perspective, is the source of everything positive in my life.

I had been living month to month as a struggling artist and healer and got to a point in my process where I remember a type of fire lighting in my soul that said "ENOUGH!" I couldn't live like that anymore, not knowing how I would make rent, feeling a deep discouragement and desperation every time I spent more than a hundred bucks on groceries. I reached out to a close friend of mine who had become a coach. I signed up for his program, invested thousands of dollars I didn't even have, and took a massive leap of faith.

That fire built the knowing that I was ready to have a new experience with life. I had crossed thresholds in my journey before—I understood the process of initiations, of going boldly into the unknown—and yet this felt qualitatively different. Choosing to engage in the world to interface with money and grow a legitimate business was a new threshold for me. With a rebel tendency, yogic lifestyle, and leaning toward the fringe and spiritual sides of life, I had resisted things that brought me more "into the world." Even so, I knew I had to participate in society in a new way if I wanted to make a larger ripple of impact.

About ten days after I invested in the coaching program, my band broke up. This band had been my focus of my life, and the falling out with my best friend with whom I had grown the project was totally heartbreaking for me. But, ten days after the band unraveled, I did my first $20,000 in sales. My entire paradigm regarding abundance—along with my entire reality—had completely shifted.

It took a deep and committed choice from deep within, along with the culmination of enough actual life experience, to genuinely claim the value of my offerings. Fast forward almost three years and I had built a strong and growing six-figure coaching business as a multi-dimensional healer/conscious business coach and had continued to grow my music as a solo artist. I was touring the United States living off what I made in the first month of the beginning of the year, which amounted to the entire amount I had made the year before. I felt like I had mastered the money game. But there was another fire burning in my heart.

At moments throughout the year, I found myself evolving out of one construct and then out of another, feeling almost alienated from previous communities with which I had once belonged. This challenged my ability to stay grounded in my business as I went through spiritual initiation after spiritual initiation being asked to let go more and more of who I thought I was. This new fire that was deepening had to do with impeccability and the desire to be in right relations with all parts of creation and to live in a flow state. I had often experienced this state when I didn't have the pressures of running a business. I had experienced a type of pendulum where I was more or less broke living in scarcity month to month to a higher end; but it was a much more demanding lifestyle as an entrepreneur. My inner artist felt a bit neglected, my activist a bit conflicted, and my inner mystic a bit at odds with money again suddenly—and yet I knew I was honing in on something. I was being guided toward refinement from the universe.

My background as a healer for over ten years, working with indigenous elders sitting in various ceremonies, mentoring with master healers, spiritual teachers and participating in many different lineages where the value systems were not focused nor emphasized on money; I kept a neutral approach to exploring it as energy. I was finally enjoying my life with much less energy expended on struggle and survival, and I wanted more of my tribe to experience this. My background as an event producer also started to culminate again, bridging many different worlds; I started to see where the gifts and shadows lived in each community. I so desperately wanted to build bridges of connection across these communities, seeing that each community had a different solutionary approach to the world's problems that we're facing, each perspective valid and beautiful. Each community had its unique gift and challenges, its different types of insight, power, influence, and its blind spots, shadows, and pitfalls.

There was the power of ayahuasca and its shadow, the power of money and its shadow, the power of sexuality and its shadows, and the power of music and its shadows. I could rant for a while offering multiple perspectives on the dynamics of light and shadow within community, but the focus of this is addressing the gifts and shadows surrounding that of money.

I found myself at the end of this tour in South Dakota sharing my music in support at an activism concert to protect the Lakota people's sacred Black Hills. This was a bridge-building concert welcoming people—both Native and non-Native—to stand together in solidarity. Indigenous leaders from many different tribes gathered together and the post-Standing Rock energy was strong, reconciling more and more relationships between Native and non-Native people recognizing the dire times we are living in and the need to work together. Earlier in the year, I had been sharing a presentation on bridging the gap between activism and entrepreneurship—a seemingly impossible bridge at the time—in the face of and in support to the Standing Rock movement. The gap between these two worlds still felt wide for me.

I was honing in on how to make peace with money and my purpose. I had learned the money game, but something still didn't sit right with me. I saw the impoverishment that a lot of Lakota people from places like Pine Ridge experienced, and it broke my heart. I had no desire to get on sales calls, I didn't want to make any money while there was an unseen and even hidden Third World community in our own backyard. I felt guilty. I felt saddened by the quality of greed in the world and the unique disparity of wealth and poverty that existed. I had felt things like this before, going from a small indigenous village in Mexico to a mansion in San Diego. For me, there is no separation between the earth narrative and the narrative of indigenous people; their struggle and the earth's struggle is the same. How they are treated is how our current model of consumerism and excessive capitalism treats the environment.

As I saw smiling faces break bread together, laughing and joking, I could see many of my other world travels flash before my eyes. All the places I had been where poor people who had deep spirituality but very little money were so loving, generous, and genuinely happy. In most of these cases, there were a couple of factors that led to this type of spiritual abundance. One Is that they were deeply connected to the land. The second is that they had a deep reverence and made offerings to something greater than themselves. The third determining factor is that they were in community. They were not isolated from one another; they belonged to a village.

So, if we had these things as a collective, materialism and status no longer has to be a replacement for any of these fulfillment factors.

I reflected about how capitalism and colonialism were completely enmeshed and that it was a huge blind spot for most entrepreneurial communities. How the heck do we start to decolonize consciousness and still participate with money? *Is that even possible,* I wondered.

I felt into how massive it could be to truly have value systems from the indigenous peoples of the earth actively implemented into how we do business in the world and the impact that could make. What would it look like to implement the Ubuntu *village philosophy of Africa* (when one receives it is utilized for the good of all, no one is neglected), or the value system of *For the next seven generations* of Native American tribes, or the Balinese philosophy of *tri hita Karana,* which translates as *right with god/goddess, right with nature and right with humanity.* These are value systems that determine the active choices made in day to day life. What could it look like to create a new culture around money? Is it possible to have profit while business regenerates nature, deepens connections between people, and strengthens our quality of life, of health, and of community? I believe so.

We have a unique opportunity *now* with things like cryptocurrency, heart-centered entrepreneurship, and the massive call to action to respond to an ever-increasing risk of losing essential aspects of our ecosystem— erosion of cultures, species extinction, and many other challenges of our time. It's time to make a new type of investment: one that doesn't just get you a return but will save the soul of humanity from the spiritual sickness of greed, worry, excess materialism, jealousy, comparison, shadow projection, entitlement, and posturing.

I once used the term "neo-pioneer" comparing the pioneers of the old world who traversed great oceans to discover new lands to that of a new pioneer that is stewarding new realms of thought, consciousness, and ultimately, culture. We must be bold enough to leave behind the old models where they still have a foot hold in our consciousness if we're going to anchor this new culture. This doesn't mean that we have to go broke! In fact, deeply claiming your purpose and value, choosing to give back, and being of service to something greater than yourself tends to bring prosperity—and not only monetarily.

We need a new culture around money, around the coaching industry, and in venture capitalism in general—one that evolves past objectifying other humans or nature.

As long as self-serving agendas drive the show, true and lasting fulfillment can't be sustained.

The temporary adrenaline hit of validation, of closing a sale, or of controlling how one is perceived by others will never replace a deep and qualitative enoughness that comes from doing the inner work. We have the opportunity to invest in projects, grow business, and create value exchange that contributes to the upliftment of humanity, protects the environment, and builds new systems that will no longer depend on money to thrive. Yep, I said it.

We need to invest money into systems where eventually we will no longer need money. We will have everything we need without stress, fear, or a false sense of control. That is freedom. And that is a fulfillment and a type of prosperity we can start to experience now.

From my perspective, the current culture surrounding money is broken. It is deeply disconnected from the earth with its hyper-focus on external success and materialism, and the current form of business as it stands as an exploitative, competition-driven model is unsustainable. The current model doesn't support all life on earth, and we're running out of time. Money is neither good nor bad; it is neutral. When stewarded with the proper intent and values, money can be used for good. To have wealth and also stay in right relations is a type of mastery that requires deep inner work.

This is the call of our times, to enter deeper into earth stewardship and to return to a village awareness of our interconnectedness as a species.

It is not enough to be successful from the old paradigm standards. We must give back. This is true prosperity.

Alokananda is a mentor, community builder, healer, and artist with
more than a decade of experience empowering individuals and
groups. Aloka has passed through
many initiations and immersive
trainings with varying wisdom
keepers, spiritual mentors, Native
and non-Native healers, entrepreneurs, and coaches and is a lineage
holder in multiple traditions. As
a mentor, he supports emerging

leaders in fortifying their authentic sovereignty, path to self-mastery,
and soul mission. Aloka is passionate about bridging the gap between
entrepreneurship and activism. For the past decade, he has also
devoted himself to learning from and consulting with different communities and solutionaries within varying fields of an emergent movement
that is catalyzing the co-creation of eco-villages. He's an advocate for
the preservation of indigenous wisdom. As ALOKA, his music and message carries a rallying call to participate in a new cultural narrative that
prioritizes heart centered living and earth stewardship. Learn more at
Alokaheart.com.

The Power of Feminine Prosperity

BY OLANA BARROS

Though most of us tend to equate prosperity with financial abundance, my journey with prosperity has unfolded in spiritual ways. I've been on all spectrums of prosperity—from being a stay-at-home homeschooling mother and feeling fulfilled in my twenties to being an entrepreneur in my thirties and forties and finding financial success. But it's not about money. It's about the *flow* of giving and receiving. I've learned lessons from over-giving, tapping into the infinite abundance within, and ultimately have found the balance between giving and receiving on all levels.

Giving has been a big part of my life—from monetary giving and material gifts to giving of my time in sharing wisdom as a mentor and my energy as a wife, mother, and leader. A lifestyle of service and generosity has always been a very vital part of my expression.

However, the energy of receiving and understanding the value of what true abundance is took a lot longer for me to master. And by doing so, I have discovered abundance that is congruent with my soul through the journey of owning my Feminine Power.

This is my unfolding story. I share it through those that have been my greatest teachers of prosperity.

MY MOTHER'S PROSPERITY CONSCIOUSNESS

I am deeply honored to walk closely with my beloved mother, holding sacred space as she slowly surrenders her physical body into the hereafter. It is profoundly transforming to witness her soul transcend her lifetime of living under the patriarchal energy. I am learning so much from her even still.

My mother grew up in humble circumstances. Her father was a farmer for a produce grower in California, and her mother was a homemaker her entire life. Their family was rich in love, but humble in finances. That deepened her desire to be financially independent, and, as an adult, she gave herself many luxuries that she desired.

Over the years, she has taught me the power of manifesting money so effortlessly, as if abundance and money love following her. She struggled financially as a single mother at times, but I never saw her go without. Even in lean times, I've witnessed her generosity.

Her financial prosperity came through her hard work and detailed organization of how she handled her funds. My mom always had what money could buy, but in her later years, her needs and desires became more simple and less materialistic.

When finances were slim, my mother would pray and ask for prosperity to come forth, and it did. *All the time.* Her deep faith and trust never faltered. My mom's generosity modeled just how much trust she's had in God and in the infinite abundance of all that is available for each of us. I've learned so much from her in this modeling and manifesting of money.

Her ability to ask, believe, and receive has been so effortless.
It's her elixir of manifesting abundance for herself.

Even in sickness, she's manifested the best of an amazing support system—recently moving into a beautiful nursing care facility in our hometown and receiving compassionate care by the staff.

She has displayed so beautifully the magic and mysteries of prosperity that I'm in awe of her soul's brilliance. Perhaps this is the first time I've seen my beautiful mama in the fullness of her essence! And what a gift she's given me in this witnessing. I am forever changed by it...and by her great love.

MY FATHER'S PROSPERITY CONSCIOUSNESS

My father has always been a man with deep, financial pockets. Coming from an impoverished family from the Philippines, he grew to appreciate the value of working efficiently for money. My dad has taught me the traditional road to financial prosperity: hard work, responsible choices, and being a wise steward. The main thing I remember from my youth is how generous my dad has always been in sharing his wealth with his family. He has taught me that while "money doesn't grow on trees," it also never runs out if we handle it correctly. He's always been very good at creating wealth and saving, and this is what I've learned the most from him.

His lifestyle and values may differ greatly from my own, but I value his wisdom because he's modeled so much stability for me throughout my years. I've never seen my dad struggle financially—ever. And that speaks volumes to me! He's doing something right for himself by understanding the energetics of money.

PATRIARCHAL INFLUENCE ON MY PROSPERITY CONSCIOUSNESS

Money has always been available to me. Both my parents taught me the value of hard work and being ethically honest with how to handle money. I never really went without. In fact, some of my friends envied our affluent lifestyle. One could say I was a bit spoiled.

It's been an adventurous financial ride since getting married at eighteen. I came into my husband's family with a very heightened prosperity consciousness. Yet, after much religious influence, I was thrust into an unfamiliar lifestyle of financial humility—one that conditioned me to believe that the love of money kept me out of heaven if I allowed it to consume me.

This was a hard pill for me to swallow. Yet, I wanted to be accepted into this family, so I adopted their beliefs in a way that didn't serve me. I gave in to many concepts that didn't feel congruent with my childhood high-mindedness, but I didn't know how to speak up for myself. Lacking self-confidence, I adopted a lifestyle for many years that kept me from my own power to create wealth.

My life as a Minister meant different priorities, which suppressed my desire to be wealthy. So I lived within our means to be "content with the little" and trust that our needs would always be met. My husband has always been a great provider for us, but it wasn't until we shifted in our own awareness that we didn't need to struggle financially to love and serve God or others.

After about a decade, my husband and I had had enough of being "content with the little" and were done with financial humility. Agreeably, we chose to do things differently. We decided to move to Las Vegas and make a new life for ourselves and our family. We did it quite efficiently and quickly, too.

We both worked very diligently. We built a very good life for our family. We bought many things for ourselves—a new home, new cars, fine clothing, exceptional education for our children, as well as all the things that they needed and wanted, and then some. We enjoyed some exciting trips, and our children got to spend summers with my mom in Hawaii, too.

After seven years in Vegas, we decided to sell our home and move back to Hawaii, yet we still desired to create a life that allowed us to have financial ease. It has been such a roller coaster ride of moving, career and job changes, ministry advancement, and lifestyle changes. We've always worked very hard, which taught us the work ethics and values in our personal life, ministry, and business that we still follow.

The polarity of financial humility to pursuing financial prosperity has been such a journey over the years. After a while, however, it took its toll on us. We found ourselves being slaves to the patriarchal system of religion, traditional patterns, and consumerism, an old paradigm that no longer resonated with us.

Driven predominantly by the masculine energy, we were diligent to fund the lifestyle we thought we greatly wanted in our twenties. We found ourselves reevaluating our values and priorities in our thirties. And in our latter forties, we've come to realize that financial prosperity and abundance holds an entirely different meaning for us both now.

MY RISING AWARENESS OF ABUNDANCE

From the early years of my awakening, I've done all the inner work of healing my wounds and clearing patterns—including the ones that I thought were blocking my financial flow. Perhaps you can relate to that on some level, as many on the higher consciousness path have embraced or encountered the teachings of creating our reality through our energetic vibration in thoughts, words, intentions, actions, and beliefs.

With that being said, I did all the typical self-development practices suggested in books written by wealth and abundance teachers who shed light on my limiting beliefs of poverty and even did mind-upgrades by listening to subliminal meditations to reprogram new beliefs of abundance and affluence. Perhaps you're chuckling at this point because you've done some or all of the same things I've mentioned, and maybe even some I didn't.

I'll never forget the very first time I was told that I needed to learn to exercise my receiving muscle more. I didn't know how to respond. But, from the onset of my emerging feminine awakening, receiving was something that my soul was greatly wanting me to learn.

I was so conditioned to believe that "It is more blessed to give than to receive." Besides, giving is natural for so many of us, especially for women. I was accustomed to give of my time and energy that came from my personal reservoir, which often left me depleted and burnt out because I was so rarely on the receiving end.

Self-love, self-care, and the energy of rest, retreat, and receiving had not been brought to my awareness until my early forties.

Can you relate? Most of us have been driven under this old system for many years.

But we can learn to *receive*—be it money, material things, affection, love, or time from others in our lives—without guilt or shame. And without feeling that we owe someone for what we receive.

Why is it so easy for us to give but not receive? When there can be no giving without receiving?

I believe that a big part of the reason is that we haven't been properly taught how to love ourselves or how to own our worth or value. I certainly wasn't taught this.

It's in a woman's human design, especially in the womb, to open up her sacred container to receive. Yet we've been conditioned to give, and give, and give, even at our own expense. The beauty of receiving allows us to deepen into our ability to intuitively trust the energy of abundance that's innate within us.

Abundance flows from connecting within. You don't have to work hard, or push, or drive, or manipulate for anything to manifest.

Creating abundance is simply connecting to our higher self—that divine part of us. Trusting in the infinite supply that already exists, seeing and knowing that which we desire to be currently present in our energy field, and being open to receiving it.

I continue to perceive life through clearer lenses. My feminine power keeps rising up to be eminent, freeing me to embody my creative power to manifest wealth and prosperity in all areas of my life from an inner connection to the abundance that exists in our universe.

Experiences of financial highs and lows brought this deeper connection and self-awareness of what truly matters to my soul—so much so that it's become an effortless alignment. I allow love and abundance to flow fully within my body, my relationships, my finances, my encounters with others, my contribution, and in my vibration.

Through being consciously present, listening to and trusting my inner voice, and allowing my soul's wisdom to guide me completely—I'm able to live freely and congruent with my soul's higher path. It took letting go of being in control—by releasing myself from the grip of fear and uncertainty, which led me to a great surrender and complete trust that my soul and the universe has my back. *Always.*

MY PATH OF EVOLUTIONARY PROSPERITY

Today, prosperity means so much more than money. One of my favorite scriptures when I was a professed Christian was from 3 John 2, "Beloved, I pray that you may prosper in all things and be in health, just as your soul prospers."

Life's experiences have revealed what true prosperity "in all things" means for me personally, and it has been through a journey of profound connection and living in alignment to my soul. I am connected to my I Am Presence, connected to All That Is, which is infinite, abundant, and always expanding.

Giving and receiving should be a more balanced flow. I consciously choose to live congruently with my higher truth of infinite abundance. When you know that infinite abundance is your divine expression, you'll no longer be in lack or limitation.

You can be open to give and receive because you understand that true prosperity is a constant flow of energy of giving and receiving.

We simply learn the rhythm of its energetic design as we ride the waves of divine abundance through a higher awareness that we are creators.

44

We are all perfect and powerful creators of our own reality. The question is: What are we choosing to create for ourselves?

There is no lack in anything. Nor is there any limitation—only the ones that we perceive in the mind.

Last year brought profound experiences of infinite receiving. Simply because I was open to it.

My soul took me on a journey of what I affectionately call my personal Goddess Immersion. I traveled and was supported by a dear soul sister who shared her home with me for three months. This opened me up greatly to understand and accept abundance in a way that has made me even more generous and overflowing with my love, energy, time, and money.

Every desire, every need, every expanding want I had was all so magnificently provided for me, and generously. Down to the details of what my heart and soul desired to experience. I am eternally grateful for this sacred time, as it has helped me to rewrite my story of abundance ever so freer.

I appreciate the path of abundance because it has brought me to this place of inner awareness that abundance—true abundance comes from the innate, infinite part of us.

All of us.

Abundance is not something we acquire or attain or even achieve.

It is our natural birthright.

It is our divine expression.

Olana Barros is a Divine Feminine Intuitive Spiritual Lightleader, teacher, author, and speaker. She champions a new breed of evolutionary women Lightworkers and change leaders. Her multidimensional mastery facilitates deep transformation in her workshops, retreats and programs.

Olana is the creatrix and founder of her transformational program, The Multidimensional Leadership Mastery, a 13-month immersion experience of hybrid, feminine principles with a cutting-edge mentorship that sets multidimensional women on course for global legacy and leadership.

With three decades of seasoned, spiritual leadership, Olana intuitively facilitates women leaders through deep transformational breakthroughs. They awaken fully to their divine wholeness, embodying their mission that catapults them to evolutionary leadership and blissful living for a new era.

She is wife to her beloved husband Kaimana for over thirty one years and mother to their four amazing children, ages 13, 22, 25 and 30. Olana and Kaimana are the co-creators and facilitators of Ascending Couples Immersion, a relationship-transformational experience for five days and five nights in Hawaii, where they support Sacred Unions and Conscious Couples who desire to transcend all relationship challenges while navigating the ascension path. This one-of-a-kind immersion attunes couples to 5D Love, multidimensional connection, conscious communication, and deepened intimacy, all for the higher purpose of their individual ascension and soul's higher calling together. Learn more at **olanabarros.com.**

Special Gift

Have you been playing small, perhaps hiding, or are afraid of the big vision you know your Soul is calling you to step into?
You are NEEDED NOW more than ever!

Visit **olanabarros.com/gift** to receive my FREE ebook,
"A Leader's Call To Rise: 6 Essential Keys to Raise Your Light For Your Tribe to Find You"

The Power and Practice of Receiving

BY RIMA BONARIO, TH.D.

My path to prosperity took a radical turn when I completely reorganized my relationship with money so I could see it as an outcome rather than a goal. This epiphany didn't come all at once. It came in bits and pieces. Like breadcrumbs on a trail, I followed each clue not knowing for sure where it would take me. The journey isn't over, but so far on the path I have gleaned Three Radical Truths About Money and Three Powerful Practices of Receiving:

Radical Truth #1: Money cannot be made, it can only be received.

> "Having your attention where you want it
> and when you want it is energetic mastery."
> —*MASTER ENERGY TEACHER LYNDA CEASARA*

I was talking with a friend who was feeling frustrated with her life. It had been several years since she left her corporate job for a more spiritual expression of her talents and gifts. She had recently graduated from a prestigious program and she was rightly proud of that accomplishment. But the program had taken its toll on her. She was exhausted, her relationship was stressed, and her health needed attention.

In her wisdom, she had given herself permission to rest and focus on her health and her relationship. However, a year had passed since graduation and she confided that she felt frustrated and stuck not having found a job or started a business. She leaned forward, looked me right in the eyes, and said with great intensity, "I need to make money, Rima!"

Her words hit me like a nuclear blast. Everything in me recoiled. "Yuck!" I thought. Nothing about it felt right in my system. Not the words, not the energy behind the words, not the stress associated with it, not the desperation I knew she was feeling. But I was oh, so familiar with all of it. These were, in fact, the words that ran around and around inside my head on a daily basis as I worked on my business.

It was a watershed moment hearing those words mirrored back to me in such a palpable way. It inspired me to shift my attention away from "making" money and instead place my attention on "receiving" money. I didn't know how I was going to do it, but I knew it had to be done. I simply had to change the way I viewed my work.

Radical Truth #2: Your Currency Is Tied to Your Current-SEE

> "You have to see it right before you
> can make it right."
>
> —TOM CRUM, AUTHOR OF THE MAGIC OF CONFLICT

We use the word currency to describe money. Walking my path to prosperity has taught the importance of widening the definition of currency to include other resources. Money is one form of currency. Love is another. And energy is yet another.

In the early days of my business, when I saw money as the only form of currency, I felt anything but wealthy. I knew I had so much of value to offer to my students and clients, but I struggled to fill my classes. At first, I thought that my program pricing had to be too high, even though it was really far too low for the amount of time and energy it required. I had yet to see time and energy as forms of currency. My knowledge and skill sets were also potent forms of currency that I just couldn't quite see. I was looking at it backwards using the money I "made" to define my worth and value as a teacher and healer.

I had deep knowledge and incredible skills honed over more than a decade as a healer and facilitator. I had studied with master teachers, making big investments in my self-development and my formal education. I worked hard to walk my talk in life. I diligently applied what I learned and become masterful in my relationship with my beloved, so much so that I was literally rolling in the currency of LOVE. And I was gaining mastery in my energy practices, which had already provided me such a huge return on my investment. In reality I was resource-rich!

I remember vividly the day I really got this.

I was working on a high-end offering for my Entrepreneur's Mastermind Course which I was supposed to pitch to executive women when a familiar doubt started choking my creativity and shaking my confidence: "Why on earth would these powerful women listen to me?" After all, I thought, they were financially successful in a way I had yet to be. In my mind, I wouldn't have much credibility with them. I took a deep breath and centered myself, asking whether that was true. The answer came back immediately: My current financial state was completely irrelevant because these women were not studying with me to make more money. They wanted help opening to their innate feminine power; they wanted to learn how to create more love and harmony in their relationships. They wanted what I had.

As this all became clear, I knew in my bones that these women would happily exchange the currency they had a lot of (money) for the currencies I was flush with (love, energy, knowledge). I literally laughed out loud it seemed so obvious once I saw it. And, just like that, all my doubt and resistance faded. I completed my mastermind homework assignment with ease that day. It was a learning I returned to again and again as I moved that project through to completion.

Radical Truth #3: People Are Really Bad at Receiving

> "I am a human being, not a human doing."
>
> —DR. WAYNE DYER

Most of us have not been trained to receive. We have taught our focus should be on giving. Output is king! Therefore, we gain our value and status (and often, it appears, money) from what we contribute, what we do, and what we make in the world. There is very little value placed on the very important aspects of being and receiving. This causes all kinds of problems in our world.

Think about it. What happens to all the giving if no one is actually receiving any of it? When people give and give and no one is there to receive, no amount of giving is ever enough. We all end up feeling drained from over-giving. Then on the flip side, if we never shift into receiving, a gaping hole opens up inside of us and our unfulfilled needs grow. Eventually these unmet needs get so big we may grow resentful and bitter, shut down or become depressed, or simply go numb.

> *When we live life in a perpetual state of giving and doing*
> *without receiving and being, we can simultaneously feel like*
> *we are "too much" and "not enough."*

Enoughness eludes us because we are stuck on one side of a two-sided dynamic. It's like sitting on a teeter totter with a friend who refuses to push off the ground, leaving you stranded up in the air. That's no fun at all. Each person needs to go up and come down, to lift and be lifted—give and receive, be and do.

Just like with an electrical current, we need to have an input and an output joined together so that the energy can make a complete circuit and, therefore, circulate all the way around. Quantum science shows us that everything is made up of overlapping fields of energy, so it stands to reason, we need to be connected to the Cosmic Current that underlies everything in order to receive. That is how we become the Source of our **resource**fulness!

> *These discoveries were only the first step. To integrate them, I*
> *used Three Powerful Practices of Receiving.*

Powerful Practice #1: Movement Creates Flow
Currency and prosperity have a relationship to movement. If we hoard money and don't circulate it, we aren't likely to experience life as enjoyable. Think Ebenezer Scrooge from the Dickens Classic, *A Christmas Carol*. To experience prosperity, we too must move. We have to enter the current and dance with it, if we want to experience it. We have a part to play.

I learned this lesson well during that same Entrepreneurs Mastermind Course. I had my high-end offering ready to beta-test and I wanted a group of ten to twelve women to sign up. I sent out one email to my list (it had forty-nine people on it at the time) and I posted about it on Facebook, and I waited. I got two sign-ups, then a couple more, but I was only at six a week before the course launched. I knew I needed to send a follow-up email to my list and also send an invite to a group of forty past students that I had. But I was dragging my feet. This was not uncommon.

My Mastermind Group lesson that week was all about connecting with the underlying energy field (Cosmic Current) that exists in the universe in order to "spread the word energetically." I love to get my *Woo Woo* on, so I was game. I did a small ceremony and pulled cards and placed them in a circle to hold the place for each of the women I wanted to call in. Then I waited, again. I knew I still needed to send more email, but I kept delaying. I wasn't in the energy of receiving dancing with the Cosmic Current, I was stuck in the energy of wishing and not taking action.

I became curious about my procrastination and used a self-guided inquiry tool to help me understand why I was waiting. I realized that I wasn't doing everything I needed to do because I was afraid the program would fail. I know that must sound backwards, but here was my unconscious belief: if it failed and I hadn't done everything I was supposed to do, then it wouldn't be a problem with the program, or the pricing, or even me as a teacher, it would be "just" a marketing issue. But if I did all the right marketing and it failed— well, I would have to face the fear that my offering wasn't good enough, or I wasn't good enough.

Ironically, by not doing the marketing work, I was all but guaranteeing the failure! Once I saw this, I became unstuck. I sent several follow-up emails, made more Facebook posts, reached out to my former students, and meditated in front of my circle of cards. Within 48 hours I had a total of 12 sign-ups and the course ended up topping out at 16 participants.

It was a powerful lesson in being committed to staying connected to the Cosmic Current and then taking the next right step. Action rooted in Intention. This is one of the great subtitles of prosperity teachings that is often overlooked. Intention without Action usually creates nothing. Action without Intention can create the wrong things.

Make a practice of doing micro-movements. When you're stuck on a big task, break it down into the smallest pieces you can. Rather than having the task "Launch a video blog," you might have the task "Google search on video blogging platforms." For me it was better to keep moving with one small task at a time: Do a ceremony, send an email, make a Facebook post, instead of Fill the Class.

Body-Based Variation:
You can take this practice into your body as well. If you are feeling stuck, take a Cosmic Dance Break. Get up off the chair and physically dance with the Cosmic Current. Practice tuning in and sensing the energy of the Universe that flows within you. Close your eyes and feel. Imagine the connection that is always already there and dance yourself open. Dance into your receptivity.

Power Practice #2: Focus on the NOW

Currency and prosperity have a relationship to time. Prosperity exists in the current moment. Our currency is given and received in the NOW.

For many of us, money worries are about a future that may never come to pass. If we tune in to the present moment instead and ask, "Is there anything I need right now that I don't have?" We'll see that the worry or anxiety we are experiencing is usually unfounded. In the present moment, there is a roof over my head, food in my fridge, clothes on my back. In the present moment, I have other forms of currency in abundance, such as knowledge, skills, love, time, and energy. In the present moment, I have enough.

Body-Based Variation:
Plant your feet on the ground and imagine roots coming down from your feet into the heart of the earth. Imagine a third very large root coming from your tailbone into the earth. Anchor all three roots in the heart of the earth. Begin to breathe in, and with each breath imagine the energy of the earth coming up into your body—like you are sipping light and energy up a straw. See that energy pooling in your pelvic bowl, infusing you with light. As the bowl fills, allow each outbreath to effortlessly carry away any energy that no longer serves you—worry, concern, fear, and guilt. Notice that there is enough energy in the earth to take care of you. In the present moment, there is always *enough*.

Power Practice #3: Be Your Own Source

Often when we are searching for prosperity some well-meaning person will ask, "What's your passion? What drives you?" And then they will suggest once you find it you should do that. But asking what drives you and then signing up to have yourself be driven by it is just more of the same old *do*-based paradigm.

A better question might be, "What fills you?" Can you imagine if you devoted yourself to a life focused on the things that nurture you and bring you alive? How would it be to find or create work that brought you pleasure and delight on a daily basis?

How open are you to pleasure in your life? How much joy can you tolerate? How much care and nurturing are you willing to accept in your life? These are critical questions when it comes to abundance. If we are unable or unwilling to see our own deservedness, we will unconsciously cut ourselves off from the Cosmic Current and find ourselves unable to receive.

This is what it means to be truly re-sourced. A true **Sorcerer** or **Sorceress** understands the need to fill oneself first and then allow the excess to overflow to others rather than trying to give from an empty well. Been there, done that. It's works out for exactly no one.

This practice gives you permission to CHOOSE YOU and what is good for you (rather than what you think everyone else thinks you should be doing). It requires trust that choosing you will best serve everyone. In practical terms, it means pausing and checking in with yourself before making any commitments. It's a chance to see if your YES or your NO is really aligned with your highest good. This takes practice. Be gentle with yourself if it is hard at first.

Body-Based Variation:

When you have a decision to make, try imagining each choice resting in one of your hands. As you consider the choices, notice which one feels lighter and which is heavier. Notice which feels more energizing and which feels draining. It may be scary to make the energizing choice at first, but the more you choose what fills you, the easier it gets!

Every path to prosperity is unique. Mine has been full of surprises and gifts. The takeaways for me are these:

- Prosperity has many forms of currency. Money is only one, albeit an important one at this time in history.
- How much currency we believe we have is a function of our Current-SEE, or how well we are able to see all of the many areas in our life where we are resource-rich.

- We are best able to see and feel our prosperity in the *now* moment.
- We can augment our sense of prosperity by moving, even in micro steps, toward our desires, toward what fills us.
- As we do what fills us, we shift into the energy of wealth, and we become the wealth we seek. We are the source of our prosperity.
- At its core, prosperity is a sensation of well-being that is based on our assessment of our resourcefulness. We must *source* ourselves first.
- As we receive ourselves as Source, we are able to give freely to others and bless the world with our gifts.

Your challenge, should you choose to accept it, is to use these practices to become an expert receiver. It is definitely worth the effort. Experience tells me magic happens when you cultivate an inner atmosphere and attitude of receiving and take aligned action. Two of the most readily available forms of currency you can increase in your life are energy and love. Source yourself and create wealth in the areas of energy and love in your life, and the money will follow.

Special Gift

Are you unconsciously blocking your financial success? Learn the 3 Keys to creating and sustaining financial sovereignty.

Download Your FREE *Financial Sovereignty Map* at **FinanciallySovereign.com** and discover what's missing from your prosperity practice. Plus, get this free bonus to go deeper: *Understanding the 5 Principles of Self-Sovereignty.*

Dr. Rima Bonario is a dream weaver, soul coach, and wild ♥ healer. Her life's work is facilitating potent processes and soulful healing practices that bring about a re-connection to our inherent, sacred wholeness. Rima speaks and teaches on women's sovereignty and awakening through her in-person and online workshops, group and private coaching programs, as well as through hands-on healing sessions. She brings her compassionate heart and thoughtful insight to her work,  weaving together a safe and sacred place for her clients to experience programs that include elements of myth and archetype, ritual and ceremony, and Soul/shadow work.

Rima's most recent offerings include body-based energy practices and explorations in the arenas of sexual sovereignty and embodied feminine presence. At its core, Rima supports women in connecting with the hidden feminine power source inside every woman's body and learning how to open to receive and conduct that power so that we can lead turned on lives of soulful delight, making the world better by our embodied feminine presence and our purposeful contributions. The work also includes a focus on intimacy in relationships, and especially supporting women in re-igniting the spark in their marriage.

Rima is passionate about her personal journey and walking the path of healing and expansion along with her beloved sister-students. Her vulnerability and deep sharing make her teaching style deeply accessible and profoundly impactful. Rima holds a doctorate in Transformation Psychology and has studied with Soul Mentor Sera Beak, Master Energy Teacher Lynda Caesara, Taoist Healing Master Mantak Chia, and Master Tantric Educators Tj Bartel and Charles Muir.

Rima resides in Las Vegas, Nevada with her husband Toby and her daughter Sophia. Learn more about Rima and her work at **rimabonario.com.**

Flowing in the Stream
of Grace and Abundance

BY ALLISON CONTE

My heart pounded as I sat on the edge of the cliff, facing away from my husband. Gathering strength from the mountain beneath me, I drew in a deep breath of courage. I knew he would be devastated by what I had to say.

With my exhale, I confessed: "I owe a bunch of money to my spiritual teacher, and I don't have enough to pay her."

The news landed with a thud, followed by an uncomfortable silence.

Instead of compensating my teacher for her role in a program that we'd created for my clients and colleagues, I'd spent the money on living expenses. I hadn't had any other work for several months, and I was worried that, if I paid her, I wouldn't have enough money to cover my share of the mortgage, food and other household bills.

"I don't know what to do," I whispered.

Now I could barely breathe. I couldn't look at my husband. The shame was hot and thick, like black tar.

Steadying myself, I allowed the heat to move through me. After months of avoiding the situation, I knew it was time to come out of hiding. The first step toward making things right was to tell the truth—first to myself, then to my husband and my teacher. But actually doing it was incredibly hard.

With a generous heart, my husband reached out to grasp my hand.

"I love you," he whispered as he held me tight. "Thank you for telling me. We'll face this together."

I melted into his arms and dissolved into tears.

My husband didn't hide the fact that he felt angry about my mistake, which would exacerbate our already precarious financial situation. Yet, in the same breath, he offered understanding, compassion and kindness.

"You're not the only one at fault here," he said, softly wiping the tears from my cheek. "Seems like you withheld the money not just because of the mortgage payment, but also because you were trying to claim some power in what has become an abusive relationship."

He was referring to my teacher's increasing hostility, dominating power plays, and verbal attacks, which he had witnessed first-hand – and which had been going on for months before money became an issue.

Waves of relief washed over me. This is what I'd married him for: his ability to speak the truth with love. The scary moment turned into a sweet one.

What happened next was not so sweet. I called my teacher to admit my mistake and promise to make it right. She responded by going on the attack—verbally and psychically. She actively lobbied to turn my own clients against me; and, worse, attempted to turn my husband against me, as well. I pulled out of the program and ended my relationship as her apprentice.

It was an intensely difficult time, one of the lowest points in my life. Over many years, I had invited this teacher into the inner core of my spiritual life, my marriage, my family, and my business. I loved her deeply, and grieved the loss intensely. In addition to losing her, I also faced the possibility of losing my home, my clients and my professional reputation. All of this, on top of being broke!

I couldn't see my way out of this breakdown.

I also couldn't see—yet—that this painful episode was the beginning of my learning about true prosperity.

The journey led me from victim/perpetrator dynamics all the way through to atonement, gratitude and Divine Love. Along the way, I learned important lessons about the misuse of power and the incredible freedom that comes with forgiveness.

DARKEST BEFORE DAWN

To fully understand my journey along the path to prosperity, let's travel a little further back in time, to a series of fateful events that led to the turning-point moment with my husband at the edge of the cliff.

In a late-night ceremony, I stood at the threshold of the Underworld. Throwing my prayer stick into the sacred fire, I stepped over a staff, ritually "crossing the line" to begin a shamanic journey that would lead straight into the heart of the Shadow.

Shadow, a term coined by Carl Jung, refers to parts of the self that have been split off and pushed aside into the hidden recesses of the unconscious. If not addressed, the Shadow can cause suffering and wreak havoc in our lives. Integrating this unconscious material leads to spiritual maturity and wholeness.

My teacher specialized in shamanic shadow-work, which was the focus of our program. As co-leaders, we had committed to doing our own work in parallel with the participants. So on this night, I was both a holder of the ceremony, and a participant in it.

On the other side of the stick, my teacher was waiting for me. "Why are you here?" she asked, the glow of the fire casting dark shadows on her face.

"I'm here to heal my relationship with money. I intend to transform my belief that there is 'not enough,' and the patterns I've developed based on that belief." As I stepped over the line in, I made a sacred commitment to address my money Shadow and asked Great Spirit to bless my journey.

I took this big step because I was at my wit's end. For much of my life, I'd had a tumultuous on-again, off-again relationship with money. I'd seen my bank account rise to great heights and fall to great lows, several times throughout my life. I was capable of attracting large sums of money, and seemingly incapable of keeping it.

For example, a few years ago, I was blessed with more than enough work, my income was higher than it had ever been, and I had recently received some inheritance money after my mother died. Financial abundance was flowing in my life.

Then suddenly, I fell ill with adrenal fatigue and was too sick to work. A big client project completed, and the work flow stopped. While my income dropped, my expenses were higher than ever: I had just moved to a new state, and was funding two homes, as well as raising two teenagers. More money was going out than coming in.

If I had known then what I know now, I would have been on my knees every day, offering prayers of gratitude that Life had provided more than enough money to allow me to take time off from work and invest in my physical health.

But instead, I panicked and focused on the familiar story of "not-enough." By the time my health improved, I'd spent all my savings and gone into debt. Again.

I desperately wanted to get off the money roller coaster, and the shamanic shadow-work journey was my ticket to a different ride.

LESSON #1: TRUST

My first lesson came immediately after returning home from the crossing-the-line ceremony.

In the mailbox, I found several checks from colleagues, who had responded to my request for funding to launch my new women's leadership program. Yay!

I sensed a *flow* in the way this support showed up; the money had come to me with ease instead of effort. I saw this as a sign that my work in women's leadership was aligned with my life's purpose and I believed that, with this alignment in place, prosperity would naturally follow.

As I drove to the bank to deposit the checks, tears of gratitude and joy streamed down my cheeks. My system filled with light. There was a subtle hum in my body, a harmonic vibrational frequency, that was new in my experience.

The hum in my body signaled a direct connection with the Source energy that moves All of Life. I had entered into a Stream of Grace and Abundance, and I was floating, effortlessly, in the flow of that stream.

In a flash of insight, I saw that my struggles with money had been especially difficult because I didn't know about the Stream of Grace and Abundance—and wouldn't have trusted it to hold me, if I had known, because I held these limiting beliefs...

- I have to work really hard, just to keep my head above water financially.
- I have to take care of myself (and everyone else!) because I'm not supported and there isn't enough for me.

These core beliefs—which are versions of the fundamental belief that *I am separate from All of Life*—had formed a pile of boulders that obstructed the Stream of Grace and Abundance. As long as these boulders were in place, the flow would be reduced to a trickle.

Excited to share this insight as well as the news of the monetary gifts that I'd received, I called my friend, Rima (a co-author in this book). We squealed, giggled, and sang together, thrilled to have received this gem of an insight in a way that could be experienced in the body and not merely understood in the mind.

The flow continued as I pulled into the parking lot of the bank. But as I stood in front of the ATM machine a few minutes later, a series of fear-based scarcity thoughts appeared in my mind: "*I don't have enough work. There won't be enough money to pay the bills. I'd better hold on to this money until I get some work.*"

In that moment, the hum in my body quieted and the flow stopped.

Convinced that the scarcity story was true, my mind went to work, searching for solutions. I recalled a conversation from the prior week, in which my shadow-work teacher told me that she regularly deposits checks from private clients into her personal account, to avoid paying taxes. Fear whispered in my ear, "*If it's okay for her, then maybe it's okay for me...*"

Meanwhile, another part of me hovered above my body and watched, from a distance, as I deposited the checks. The gifts from my colleagues went into my women's leadership account...and a check for the shadow-work program went into my personal account.

As soon as the check disappeared into the machine, my body went weak. I felt *awful.*

Time slowed way, way down.

In slow-motion replay, I saw what had just happened in a series of distinct steps:

1. A fear-based thought entered my mind.
2. My consciousness contracted, stopping the flow.
3. I fell out of the Stream of Grace and Abundance.
4. I took action from this state of fear-based contraction.
5. My body signaled that something was wrong.

My body's signal was so strong that I instantly realized my mistake. As soon as I could, I transferred the money into the right account – and immediately felt relief. I took a deep breath and thanked the Divine for this lesson.

Lesson #1
The path to prosperity requires that I trust in Life. When I withhold trust and act on fear-based thoughts, I drop out of the Stream of Grace and Abundance.

Prayer #1
I am grateful for the Divine Life-force energy that flows through All of Life, including my life. I release all beliefs that I am separate, that I am not supported, and that there isn't enough for me. I relax, trust and allow myself to flow in the Stream of Grace and Abundance.

LESSON #2: TRUSTEESHIP

As with many insights, the moment of realization is illuminating, enlightening, enlivening and life-changing.

It's sexy!

For a minute.

And then comes the real work: integrating and embodying the knowledge by taking radical responsibility for our mistakes, cleaning up the mess we've made, and changing our behavior. This part of spiritual growth—facing the Shadow, owning the self-deception, and transforming destructive patterns—can be so daunting that many people run the other way, or secretly hope to be rescued.

When we turn away from our personal work, Life presents the same lesson again and again, with increasingly painful consequences. In Life School, we always have a choice: Learn, or repeat the lesson.

For me, a single moment of revelation at the ATM machine was not enough to break the spell of scarcity. Thoughts of "not enough" continued to haunt me, cutting off the flow. Work and income continued to elude me.

As my fear intensified, I took more fear-based actions, creating a downward spiral that led me to what was, for me, rock bottom: withholding the money from my teacher.

At this point, my money Shadow had negatively affected my teacher, my husband, my clients and my children (who wouldn't have the benefit of my support for college). I could no longer tell the story with a straight face that scarcity was happening *to me*; I knew that it was happening *by me*.

I was determined to make things right—and learn my lessons in a way that would stick.

Day after day, I sat in meditation, and prayed for Spirit to guide me.

One morning as I sat in meditation, I was shown a memory from years ago, words of wisdom passed on to me by a yoga teacher: "The yoga is not always on your mat," she said. "Sometimes, the yoga is in your checkbook."

The first time I heard this message, I nodded my head in agreement, but did not actually follow the instruction. This time, I received it as a precious gift, wrapped in gold.

Holy wow. A major tectonic plate shifted in my system. *The Goddess is in my checkbook!!??*

To be sure I got the message, Spirit offered another clue right away. As came out of meditation, I saw a tiny little book that had recently been given to me by a neighbor. I picked it up and opened it to a random page.

> "All wealth belongs to the Divine and those who hold it are trustees, not possessors...In your personal use of money, look on all you have as belonging to The Mother. Be self-less, scrupulous, exact, careful with detail, a good trustee. Always consider that it is Her possessions, and not your own, that you are handling."
>
> —SRI AUROBINDO, THE MOTHER

A chill swept through my body in response to this Truth. As a mystic, doing anything as an act of service to the Divine is more motivating, for me, than doing it for my own sake.

Shaking, I got on my knees and committed to be a good trustee of the Goddess' money.

Of course, making a promise is easier than keeping it. I have a master's degree from a prestigious business school, but I knew that my professional credentials would not qualify me for the role of "good trustee." I would have to earn it by getting serious about reeling in spending, paying bills on time, reducing debt, and being honest with myself about all the ways in which I had stepped out of divine alignment with money.

I realized that trusting the flow of Grace and Abundance was necessary, but not sufficient, to pull me out of the dark hole I was in. I also needed to align my system (both energetically and with my actions) with that flow.

This part of the journey was neither easy, nor quick. My commitment to be a good trustee of Divine resources challenged and stretched me in ways that I didn't want to be challenged or stretched. But I leaned into the discomfort and did the work anyway.

My husband and I held weekly "business meetings" in which we reviewed the numbers, wrote the checks, and revised the budget. We cut back on spending. We rented a room in our house to help cover the bills. We even considered selling our home.

In addition to this "yoga in the checkbook" approach, I did the inner work to support a more sustainable prosperity: I practiced gratitude. I cleared psycho-spiritual blocks and limiting beliefs. I used my magic. And I learned to ask for—and receive—help.

Lesson #2
To stay in the Flow of Grace and Abundance, I must be trustable with the resources that Life brings to me.

Prayer #2
All resources belong to the Divine. I commit to being a good steward of all resources that are entrusted to me.

RECEIVING MIRACLES

Because I'd addressed the belief that I have to do it all myself, I was now more open to receive assistance on my journey–without which, I would not have found my way through from Darkness to Light.

Help flowed to me, in beautiful ways: My husband rubbed my feet while I balanced my books; my sister-friends offered energy-work sessions; a new spiritual teacher came into my life; my mentors reflected back to me the incredible Light of my Being-ness; and my spirit guides orchestrated opportunities and miracles along the way.

Since I started practicing the first two lessons, my path to prosperity has been paved with Divine guidance and miracles. Here's but one example:

I struggled to figure out how I would pay the debt to my former teacher. Six months after the mountaintop conversation, I had not found a solution.

One day, as I was throwing away junk mail, I stopped in my tracks: In my hand was an offer to refinance our home. Offers like this had started arriving in the mail almost daily, with increasing volume—much in the same way that Harry Potter's invitation to Hogwarts School filled his step-parents' mailbox to overflowing. But I had been throwing them away, as Harry's step-father had done.

I threw them away because my husband had refused to consider refinancing our home. He (rightly) did not want to use our personal shared finances to pay off my business debt.

In this moment, I realized that I had been ignoring messages from Spirit! So I asked my husband to reconsider and, this time, he said yes.

When the new mortgage loan came through, it was in the exact amount of debt that I owed—to the penny. It was also the same amount of equity that I had put down on our house before we were married, which meant that we did not have to use shared equity for my business debt, after all. With auspicious timing, I paid off the shadow-work program, in full, in the same month that it had originally been scheduled to end.

Looking back at this experience, it's clear that the breakup with my teacher was a direct answer to my prayers, the fulfillment of the intention I set as I crossed the line in the shamanic ceremony. I'd placed an order, and the universe delivered. For that, I'm unendingly grateful.

Of course, I did not consciously ask for a shit-show. But the lessons that came with this experience were an invaluable opportunity for me to transform a lifetime of struggle into enduring blessings.

LESSON #3: SHARING

I think of Trust as the water that flows in the stream of Grace and Abundance, and Trusteeship as the stream's solid, earthen banks. A stream without banks to contain it is a stagnant swamp—there is no flow. With banks, the stream flows.

The path to prosperity requires **both** Trust (faith and flow) **and** Trusteeship (commitment and discipline). Magic and prayers are stronger—and more effective—when they are paired with committed, aligned action.

When we learn to be both trusting and trustable, we are primed for the next step on the path to prosperity.

As Trust and Trusteeship grow, our exchange with Life expands, and prosperity increases. The more we allow ourselves to receive, the more we have to give...and the more we give, the more we can receive. It's a beautiful dance. We receive by taking in nourishment and resources, and we give by sharing our time, talents and treasures; creating something of value; or expressing gratitude.

Exchanging with Life in this way is considered one of the primary "rights of being" that are granted to all humans, according to some Native American teachings, which suggest that an essential ingredient in a healthy exchange with Life is sharing.

My current shamanic teacher, from the Apache lineage, tells the story of her grandmother, who defined prosperity as *having enough to share.* At the physical level, this means having enough resources to meet basic needs, plus some reasonable wants, with some left over to give to others. Gifting and tithing are fundamental practices associated with this teaching, and a central way of life for many Native American tribes.

Beyond the physical level, this conception of prosperity encourages us to contribute in an intangible way, by sharing our personal gifts and knowledge with others. For me, this serves as a good reminder that, when I am flowing in the Stream of Grace and Abundance, I have more capacity to give in this way, offering my wisdom in service to the highest good for all.

Lesson #3
The more I grow in my exchange with Life, the more
I am able to contribute to others.

Prayer #3
I am grateful for all the ways that Spirit provides.
Abundance flows to me easily and, in gratitude, I happily
share with others.

THE GREATEST PROSPERITY OF ALL

Recently, a dear friend brought his family, who were visiting from California, to our mountain home in Colorado for a Sunday afternoon visit. Soon after they arrived, an unexpected spring snow storm hit. As they were attempting to leave, their car spun off the road; it had become impassable in under two hours. They called us to come and get them.

When everyone was back safely at the house, my husband and I cooked a big meal, built a fire, poured hot toddies, and made up the guest beds. Our two families feasted, shared stories, played parlor games, and listened to music until late in the night. The one child among us snuggled up next to the fire with the cat, falling asleep to the sounds of laughter.

The greatest prosperity of all, according to the Apache grandmother, includes *and transcends* the sharing of resources or even skills and talents. The most prosperous among us, she said, are blessed with enough time and energy to share, with friends and family, the things that are most meaningful in life: laughter and tears, joys and sorrows, gains and losses, and lessons learned.

In other words, prosperity means Love.

Allison Conte serves as a bridge between the worlds of work and spirituality. She is an executive coach, organizational consultant, author, and speaker—and a mystic, intuitive, oracle, and spiritual guide. Allison's mission is to help humanity live in harmony with All of Life in ways that honor the Sacred, balance the Masculine and Feminine, and wield power wisely. She works with leaders, coaches, consultants, and entrepreneurs who are committed to being a force for good in the world and who are ready to do the deep inner work required to embody this purpose. As founder of Sophia Leadership, Allison is focused on bringing the Feminine principle into balance with the Masculine principle in organizational leadership and culture. The Sophia Leadership program helps women to lead with more of their innate Feminine essence so they can generate true, sustainable success for themselves and their organizations. Allison has served on the faculties of the Gestalt Institute of Cleveland and the Integral Center, and worked as a master executive coach in Case Western Reserve University's Weatherhead School of Management Executive Education Program. Although she considers her spiritual path to be mystical and universal (honoring all wisdom traditions), Allison is deeply devoted to the Sacred Feminine and was ordained as a priestess in the Sophia Lineage in 2013. For nearly twenty years, she has studied intensively with master shamans, spiritual teachers, energy-work masters, and healers. She holds a master's degree in Positive Organization Development from CaseWestern Weatherhead School of Management, and a bachelor's degree in Journalism from the University of Colorado. She is a certified Spiritual Intelligence Coach. Allison lives in Boulder, Colorado, with her husband, a Christian pastor who captured her heart by welcoming the return of the Divine Feminine in his own tradition. Learn more: **www.sophia-leadership.com** and **www.allisonconte.com**

Igniting a Sacred (R)evolution™ a.k.a. A New Bottom Line of Love

BY LAINIE LOVE DALBY

"Money is like water. It can be a conduit for commitment, a currency of love. Money moving in the direction of our highest commitments nourishes our world and ourselves. What you appreciate appreciates. When you make a difference with what you have, it expands...Let your soul inform your money and your money express your soul."

— *LYNNE TWIST,* FROM THE SOUL OF MONEY

We are at a crucial point in human history, a great turning of the ages, when all of our deep gifts, resources, and attention are needed to help gracefully usher humanity into the next century and beyond. The world is experiencing a global awakening, and more and more people, especially women, are choosing to participate in this renaissance of spirit and substance. We are in the collective fire now, being transmuted and alchemized by the flames in a great unveiling.

Together, in diverse sacred circles, ephemeral temples, councils, and communities we are being invited to rise to the occasion of a world in crisis. We are being challenged to burn away what is no longer serving us with this fierce feminine flame so that we may midwife the new paradigm into being. That's probably why you're here inside the pages of this book, Beloved...

We are alive at a pivotal moment when systems are crumbling, the levels of suffering are becoming nearly insurmountable, and we are deeply submerged in an age of separation and scarcity. The vast majority of us have forgotten the sacredness of life. We've forgotten how to love and are consumed by fear instead. We've lost respect for each other and our Great Mother Earth. Life has been disregarded in favor of profit, greed, and personal agendas. Just in America alone, despite enjoying a level of prosperity that would have been unthinkable to our ancestors, many of us are still plagued by delusions of scarcity, competitive mindsets, rampant greed and self-centeredness. From this place, we can easily get caught in the unconscious feedback loop of *"There's not enough," "I'm not enough," "I'll never have enough"*—even, at times, within the women's entrepreneurial community that is meant at its core to help us heal through this.

We have lost touch with the ancient earth-honoring systems going all the way back to goddess worship and indigenous shamanism—the original spirituality—and instead have bought into the modern-day patriarchal systems that have suppressed these sacred ways for more than three thousand years. One serves Life, while the other serves greed. One serves the bottom line of love while the other serves the bottom line of money. One operates in the unseen realm, the other in the seen, middle world reality. One is sacred, the other profane. One is connected to the seemingly extraordinary, the other the ordinary. One is based on abundance and surplus while the other is based on scarcity. One serves humanity, the other serves the individual. One involves the metaphysical and magical, the other strictly physical and material. One is based on the interconnection and interdependence of all Life, the other on the delusion of separateness.

Most unfortunately, Beloved, we have found ourselves firmly ensconced in the latter paradigm. This age of separation is closely related to our alienation from nature, our own bodies and the Sacred Feminine. It has severed us from our own souls and our souls' physical address in this lifetime, our holy body temples. On top of that we are collectively starving for depth, meaning, and purpose largely because we don't value the inner life in our culture. Our current systems don't foster our wholeness or encourage our innate brilliance and Spirit to flourish. In most cases they crush us and drain the life and light out of our eyes. They keep us small, tamed, and in line. At their worst, they perpetrate violence that limits our potential and ability to become who we're meant to be in this lifetime.

Luckily, once we wake up to this reality, we realize that we always have a choice to serve and protect Life instead of just a self-serving agenda.

Instead of just asking "How can I personally prosper and achieve abundance," we must ask now, "What will be for the nourishment and benefit of all beings?"

This is the opportunity and the challenge we have before us. The question is: *Are we willing to do what it takes to co-create the new world we want to see? Who do we want to show up as in this grand unfolding, both individually and as a collective?*

What if we were to live into the ancient system rooted in love while we dismantle the patriarchal systems of oppression that are ready to die away and be reborn anew?

It is my prayer that we show up authentic to our core and unapologetic for this consciousness-raising journey. That we bring resilience and determination to our vision. That we turn toward our shadows, shining light into the darkness and ignorance in the world, most of all our own. That we examine our privilege, our access, and our entitlement. That we show up to do the right thing with diligence and daily work. That we speak truth to power with the strength of our fierce feminine voices when others are abusing their power, standing in our convictions and saying *"NO, not on my watch is this going to happen in my country, or in my hometown, or in my community, to my brothers, sisters, or beloveds."* That we dismantle and alchemize who we thought we were in order to become who we're meant to be. That our latent gifts and abilities from ancient, present, and future selves continue to emerge now in service to the greater good. That we come into our power and sovereignty without hesitation or holding back from fear of being burned (again). That we instead fearlessly put our feet into the fire and remain willing to dance, engaging and maintaining full presence even as we burn, baby, burn in the white hot flames of transmutation.

I pray that we choose to rise as Warriors of the He(art) now.

Most of all I pray that we come home to the body, to the earth, to all sentient beings and the he(art) of what matters most—including this one wild and precious life we've been given.

I deeply believe that each and every one of us matters and that we're here to do something that matters. We have a responsibility to live into our (r)evolutionary potential for the good of all. We must each add our unique stroke to the collective masterpiece, or else it will be forever lost. Like cells in the body, we each have a divine assignment to serve the greater functioning of the whole: the body of humanity. We are the vision carriers of this new world that we want to see in which basic human rights and dignity are universally respected and upheld. We have the opportunity now to be embodied leaders helping to heal the world with purity of heart and intention, staying true to our authentic essence. This is at the core of all I do and is how I choose to define the conversation around abundance, prosperity, and "success."

We are walking stardust—every single living being—regardless of race, class, nationality, religion, or species. It is our true nature to *shine*. Shining together, there is an interconnected constellation of us just like the stars shining brilliantly in the night sky: flooding the house of humanity with light, each a cosmic and radiant node in our interconnected Web of All Life. My life's work is to help us all do just this: SPARKLE SHAMELESSLY®. It's allowing our spiritual magnificence to come forth, our soul essence, the reality and raw truth of who we are. It's our unique #SOULSPARKLE and medicine that only we can bring to the world. To Sparkle Shamelessly is to be *lit* up, *turned* on, *blazing* true. It's feeling our full life force energy and being filled with aliveness. It is being wholly merged with the holiness of our true essence. It's the full embodiment of our authentic radiance. It's remembering who we truly are and claiming our worth. It's standing in our highest power and artistry, serving Life. It's knowing we are enough just as we are, and that we are whole and sovereign. It's having a wealth of inner resources to be grounded, anchored, and centered in the midst of our chaotic world. Most of all, it is taking a stand for deep nourishment and *flourishing for all*.

This is what true prosperity looks like to me.

But this isn't where we are currently. Instead, the outside world has us numbed out and confused with all the wrong things to keep us from diving into the deep core and truth of who we are. We have had our attention stolen by countless distractions from what matters most, we have had our power pushed down and our greatness repressed, and we have had our life force squandered. We have bought into the patriarchal myths of lack and unworthiness, and we have knowingly gone along with the toxins pumped into our daily lives through our consumer culture, the unjust practices inflicted upon our fellow humans, and the injection of life-killing ingredients into our food system and our earth. Countless crimes against humanity happen each day, yet we turn the other way, going about our lives. We have fallen asleep...and keep hitting the snooze button when the world is screaming at us to *wake up!*

We have a tendency to collude unless we remain vigilant and fully awake. When we fall back asleep, we can become stuck in these harmful and insidious systems of oppression flavored with sexism, racism, greed, classism, homophobia, and the disease of separation that are fueled by the bottom line of money in our world. I have been sickened and disgusted, with bile literally rising in my throat some days, by the diseases that have even seeped into our spiritual "healing" communities and the business of "spiritual" entrepreneurship and other "female empowerment brands." Even my own. In the beginning of my spiritual journey there were moments where I slipped into unconsciousness and wanted to just exist in my high vibes and keep it all "love and light," since it's easier than remaining fully awake to the suffering, rampant white supremacy, and disregard for life that is happening all around us. But I quickly realized that if you're focused only on increasing positivity in your life and feel that all is well in our world as is, you're truly not looking deeply enough. We must fearlessly unearth and heal through the shadows and darkness in order to step into our full light or else we remain in a state of spiritual bypass, living half-lives.

When our need for security wins out around the conversation of prosperity and we follow the status quo, we only fall into a deeper slumber. We become deadened to life. My own mother even looked away when my greedy father started getting into illegal business dealings. She liked her monthly allowance and our extravagant beachside condo and copious luxury items more than the truth that was staring her in the face. But then the veil of illusion lifted and the shaky foundation fell to pieces. My father went to jail. Our family went from riches to rags overnight and lost all of our worldly possessions, including our home, to bankruptcy. My parents divorced and I started high school with my father's mugshot plastered all over the front page of the local paper. It wasn't the best entree into adolescence.

Years later, I too had constructed an entire life for myself that resembled a flimsy house of cards, a desperate picture of what I thought I was supposed to have, want, and be in my life instead of getting deeper in touch with the truth of who I really was and why I was here. Success and prosperity meant something very different to me then. It was all about external appearance, worldly possessions, and climbing the linear ladder of success to the next highest rung. I was wasting away my precious 112 hours per week focused on the me instead of the we.

A decade ago, I experienced what I like to call my 'quarter-life crisis.' It gave me the intimate firsthand understanding that hoarding your money, nursing delusions of grandeur, being greedy, acting selfishly, and not giving back are principles that lead you directly into poverty—not only financial poverty, but *love* poverty, friendship poverty, fulfillment poverty, and spiritual poverty.

For the ten years prior to this, I was lost in the sticky lala lands of darkness and illusion on an arduous and entangled journey in the material realms of fame, sex, vanity, greed, and artifice. I lived as an international artist, celebrity stylist, avant-garde fashion designer, and professional Dominatrix, to name just a few of my many incarnations. While entertaining my ego by playing in these largely loveless realms, I became a selfish, shutdown shell of myself. Just another lost bitchy, narcissistic diva posing for the camera. I was a full-blown hedonist and fame monster who was totally bankrupt—financially, spiritually, and emotionally—with a permanent neon sign flashing "CLOSED" over my heart. I was obsessed with the surface and blind to the essential inner and outer truths that rule our deepest existence and greatest fulfillment.

My life had become devoid of meaning, and I had lost my personal anchor to what really mattered. I wanted to die, straight up, and was brought to the precipice of suicide on my Brooklyn loft rooftop. Luckily, through Divine intervention, that fateful evening also led me through the portal of whole systems transformation and started me off on the spiritual path at a two-year interfaith seminary program. It was the powerful pivot point that literally saved my life and helped me flip my riches to rags story to now being deeply *soul rich.*

The biggest lesson I learned from this chunk of my life journey is that we're here on this planet to give and not to get. We are here to love and be the presence of love itself.

We are here to discover who we truly are and deliver our divine legacy. We are here to inhabit our *aliveness* and share our deep gifts to meet the world's deep needs. We are here to serve our fellow sentient beings by offering what I like to call our **#LoveCurrency,** not just to acquire lots of shiny new toys, electronics, worldly possessions or middle-world reality markers of abundance and success.

I made the radical and life-saving shift from egotistic individualist, constantly saying "gimme what I want," to devoted sacred activist proclaiming "lemme serve you with what you need." I believe it's our time to move from "I" and "ME" to "US" and "WE" as a global village. (Just think, there's an "I" in the word *illness* and a WE in the word *wellness!*) However, until we awaken to our interconnectedness with all beings—until we honor the Spirit and Divine spark in all things and act from this higher consciousness —we cannot do so.

Let us awaken from our collective amnesia now, answering the call of the Goddess and Mother Gaia whispering her ancient prayers deep into our wombs and hearts, Beloved. This is the time of remembering, coming home, awakening, and returning to who we are and who we've always been.

I believe what we need now is a Sacred (R)evolution™ of love and reverence for self, each other, the planet, and the Web of All Life. What we need now is a new bottom line of love aimed at restorative justice, collective healing, and fierce liberation.

The social entrepreneurial community often talks about the triple bottom line of people, planet, and profit. A positive start, but not even this trifecta truly gets at the root of what is missing in our world: *love*. And I'm talking about *true love*, heart-broken-wide-open-with-pain-and-grief-for-the-suffering-in-our-world *love*, unconditional *love* not prescribed by skin tone or class rank or social standing, radical *love* for all, starting with ourselves.

Reconnection is the medicine that is most greatly needed in our world today.

Reconnecting to our own bodies, to each other, to our Mother Earth and to the greater Web of All Life: that's why the Sacred (R)evolution™ is the powerful anchor for my work in the world at this pregnant moment. How we show up for ourselves, each other, and the planet is what comes first. Serving *Life*. And I believe that this sacred reconnection will bring an end to the rampant violence in our world—especially the violence perpetrated against women, girls, BIPOC and the LGBTQIA population due to greed and the bottom line of money. That's why it's essential for us to create a new bottom line of love instead of focusing on immediate financial gains and return on (financial) investment. Won't you join me, Beloved?

Honoring all Life as sacred is an essential new feminine paradigm and pathway to true prosperity for all.

Attaining this new vision of prosperity is so essential because **we are being invited to plant seeds that will grow into future nourishment, serv-**

ing *Life* **and the next seven generations.** This is what is needed now to truly help us heal, grow, transform, and create a nourishing, earth-honoring culture around us once again.

My invitation to you is to unhook from mass consciousness and the negative stream of our culture of violence, hatred, and sexism. Instead, let's lean into the Divine Feminine principles for regeneration and sustenance as a holistic and healing alternative and allow them to be supported by the existing Divine Masculine principles.

Instead of trading hours for money, let's focus on the re-genesis of our society.

We have the potential to become instruments for the transformation we need in the world NOW. We can create a new bottom line of love TOGETHER by:

- Upholding the basic human rights of all sentient beings as the top priority in all of our affairs involving currency and otherwise, whether business, family, society, or pleasure.
- Being intentional about where we place our precious life force energy (to help make the world a better and more sustainable place for everyone in the global village).
- Planting energetic seeds that we can harvest for years to come through living in right relationship and harmony with the greater good, letting our actions protect all Life.
- Practicing gratitude and tending to all that we already have.
- Deeply nourishing our physical bodies & the body of Mother Earth FIRST, honoring the source of all Life and tapping into the healing metaphors and wisdom in nature.
- Gathering in sacred circle and tending to the soul of community (especially the ancient sisterhood lineages) so we can re-member and create powerful vortices of healing, like acupuncture needles on Mother Earth.
- Practicing actual diversity and inclusivity (especially with BIPOC, disabled, and LGBTQIA individuals) by creating true bridges for healing.
- Creating new paradigms of leadership—moving from hierarchical leadership to shared leadership and collaboration—since we will rise together.

- Returning to indigenous values instead of capitalist values.
- Honoring and incorporating the wisdom of our own indigenous ancestral lineages instead of engaging in cultural appropriation.
- Having clarity of vision and purpose, fierce passion, and commitment to do the right thing.
- Circulating our **#LoveCurrency,** showing up in service with our deepest gifts to sustain Life from a place of deep heart and integrity.
- Setting our sights on the long game of *whole systems transformation* for our world and all its crumbling outdated structures.
- Upholding the sacredness and equality of all beings by remembering our true nature and oneness.
- Practicing nonviolent communication and aiming to create no harm, including with Mother/Lover Earth.
- Leaning into more wisdom and less effort by taking ample time for sacred rest & recharging in our fast paced world (i.e. doing less and being more)
- Focusing on creation as an antidote to destruction by leaning into the wisdom of life-death-rebirth cycles, the seasons, planetary rhythms, and the moon cycles.
- Dreaming the new world into being as a collective force field for good through co-creativity, bartering, collaboration, cooperation, trading, gifting, partnering, and new forms of weaving progress while still retaining our sovereignty.

We need fierce, sober courage now to do step into these practices in the face of such injustice and upheaval around the world. That's why I've been carrying the torch for the Fierce Feminine in the world: we need to not only tap into our deep inner well of compassion but also moral outrage at the grave destruction and violence happening all around us. The Dark Feminine Goddesses—such as the skull-wearing Hindu goddess Kali, the Hawaiian volcano goddess Pele, and the lion-headed Egyptian goddess Sekhmet— came to me early on in visions and have been fierce guides for me, carrying me on the journey of discovery and transformation through sacred rage, deep inner alchemy of the shadow, life/death/rebirth mysteries, the creator/ destroyer paradigm, annihilation, and the sustainable burn.

They have helped me to *lean in* instead of turning away...for now is a time of staying *with*, standing *with*, withstanding and *turning towards* what's painful and dark, and who is suffering the most. We must crack open our hearts to the depths of compassion that we're capable of holding now, fortifying and strengthening our heart chakras for the journey.

We are here to be He(art) Warriors coming from the heart with our deep gifts and unique medicine and sharing that on behalf of the good of the whole body of humanity and the next seven generations. We are leading the Sacred (R)evolution™ together. We are expanding into the next level of love and service we want to show up for in the world. We are being mindful of where we are out of alignment and integrity, from white privilege to unconsciously following the status quo. We are seizing the courage to birth our love into the world. We have a moral responsibility to show up fully now.

Imagine if instead of money, the most familiar currency was love—that it trumped all others and came first above all other human exchanges? "Currency" comes from the Latin "currere," meaning "to flow" or "to run". "Current" is from the same root and it means "a flowing" or "a running" (like a river). "Currency" is also "the act of being accepted, passed and circulated from person to person"—a medium of exchange that flows between people—and it was only in 1699 that the meaning of the word began to include "circulation of money." Before that, it just meant "a condition of flowing."

Money is energy, just as love is energy. Both are a means of exchange and utilized for creating value in our lives, creating lasting connections and consequences for the future of all parties involved. With both, our aim is to be *in the flow* of giving and receiving, like the ocean tides rolling in and out of the shoreline. Like the infinity loop in my shamanic healing he(art)work on the cover of this book—swirling in and back out, around and around continuously, never ceasing.

Try thinking from the perspective of **#LoveCurrency** and making love the new bottom line. See how that might influence your decision, spur more creative thinking for alternate solutions, and add to the betterment of planet Earth, for it is the only home we've got. As one of my dear mentors, Jean Houston, has shared, "Humankind must be transformed through *loving*. Love or Perish."

If love were our bottom line, would we allow for almost half the world—over three billion people—to live on less than $2.50 a day?

If love were our bottom line, would one percent of the United States control over forty percent of the nation's wealth?

If love were our bottom line, would we allow landfills to become oozing cesspools of greed and consumption pockmarking Mother Earth's surface?

If love were our bottom line, would 795 million people around the world not have enough food to live a healthy and active life?

If love were our bottom line, would there be over 30 million people enslaved around the world, mostly women and girls, in the human trafficking trade?

I deeply believe that someone out there needs us. The question is: *Are we ready to live our lives so they can find us? Who do we want to BE in the world? What songs do our souls yearn to sing? Where do we want to channel our valuable life force energy?*

We have the opportunity now to help change the tides, to shift the consciousness of humanity to one of unity, to come back to the he(art) of what matters most and to remember that love is one of the greatest forms of currency that we have to give & receive.

I propose that instead of following the money, we follow the energy of what has he(art) and meaning for us instead: the deeper call, the symbols, the synchronicities, the "truth bumps" running up our arms and the undeniable tears, the full bodied yes pulsing in every cell in our bodies, the things that bring us deep joy or heartbreak.

The beauty of this is that when we talk about **#LoveCurrency** we are also speaking about the access that we have to a pure channel of love flowing through us. We are all vessels for Spirit/God/Goddess/Universe/the Muse/Great Mystery/Insert-your-own-here. *How can you purify and clear away what no longer serves you? How can you be a clear channel for what wants to be birthed through you out into the world?*

Without the meaning and value we ascribe to it, a $100 bill is just a piece of paper (a tree sourced from the earth, a gift from the Great Mother)! We must remember that money is a human invention after all, but love has always been and will always be. It is the one constant sure thing. Imagine if we were to make this our new currency! As Marianne Williamson has said, "We experience who we really are, and what it is we're meant to do, in any moment when we pour our love into the Universe."

We have the opportunity to be living, breathing chalices of love in the world, overflowing with the unconditional, radiant, never-ending

divine nectar of love from our he(art). That is my deepest prayer for you, Beloved.

He(art) Warriors and #LoveCurrency are essential new definitions for the 21st century. We are offering the creative expression sourced deep from within our core, our unique gifts that only we can give our planet, our own deep medicine in service to the world's deepest needs. We're living our lives as a sacred prayer. We're adding our addition to the great cosmic master-piece. We're sharing the true wealth we have to offer. What we're born to deliver. Our delicious Dharma. Our Divine Destiny. Our soul whispers. A currency of the he(art). It's why we're alive here, now.

Coming from the he(art) and a new bottom line of love is the only way our world is going to change and heal. I also believe that it's the overall key to our fulfillment, prosperity, the flourishing of all Life!

So, Beloved...

Let us collectively move from ME to WE.

Let us chase DEEP MEANING instead of MONEY.

Let us SERVE and PROTECT LIFE in all our endeavors.

Let us PUT OUR LOVE INTO ACTION to halt the dark night of the globe starting TODAY.

Let us be WARRIORS OF THE HE(ART) delivering our deepest gifts to the world.

Let us move toward our SACRED (R)EVOLUTIONARY POTENTIAL for the good of all.

And most of all let us SPARKLE SHAMELESSLY® and flood the house of humanity with light!

Special Gift

Visit **lainielovedalby.com** to receive your FREE #SOULSPARKLE Starter Kit to begin the journey today! It's a 13 day experiential course to claim your worth, embrace radical acceptance and gain the courage to Just be YOU!

Lainie Love Dalby is an embodied leadership mentor, transformational catalyst, visionary sacred artist, modern-day soul alchemist, rabble rouser for the Goddess, fierce leader of women's empowerment, metamorphic magician, human potential maven, deep wisdom walker, and blazing brave He(art) Warrior. She's on a mission to free human spirits that have been oppressed and devalued to *Sparkle Shamelessly*® and step into their authentic power—especially women, girls and the LGBTQIA community.

As a spiritual thought leader with her own brand of multimedia ministry, she is using style, sass and the sacred to dismantle old systems, ideas, and ways of being that promote separateness and limit our full (r)evolutionary potential. She is also deeply passionate about ending the violence we perpetrate against each other and our own bodies by reminding us of our inherent divinity within and helping to bring the sacred feminine back into balance in our own lives and the world.

Like a modern-day medicine woman, her ultimate goal is to help us feel more comfortable in our own skin and remember who we truly are and why we're here at this most powerful time in human history. To this end, she is the founder of The Sacred (R)evolution™, gathering women and the LGBTQIA community in sacred circle to facilitate deep healing, sacred play, soul growth, and alchemical transformation through her signature immersion experiences like Ignite the Fierce Feminine Within, Sovereign Sisters Rising 7-month Initiation into the Fierce Feminine, global retreats, and other sisterhood initiatives. Embark on your own journey at **lainielovedalby.com** and on Instagram **@LainieLoveDalby.**

Self-Worth as the Portal to Prosperity

BY DANA DAMARA

I remember sitting with my mother while she smoked cigarettes after dinner and paid our bills. Her process consisted of writing checks, balancing the household checkbook, putting the bill in the envelope, handwriting the addresses, licking the stamp, and putting it in the mailbox for the morning mail.

She seemed to be always complaining about how there was never enough...never enough time, never enough money, never enough of *anything*. And I remember feeling sad that she saw it that way. I never felt scared that we would be broke, but I never felt like we had enough. I felt rushed with time, like I always had to be the first one at an event. I mean, I may not get a seat or a spot! I felt like I needed to grab every opportunity that came my way in fear of not having another opportunity come up again—ever. I saved pennies for a rainy day—one that never really came, to be honest. And, I never, *ever*, felt good enough in anything I did or tried to do. That was my truth for a *really* long time.

Even when I pay my bills today, I sometimes feel that same tightness I could sense in my mother when she was doing the bills. Because "paying our bills" is a form of energy exchange and shows up in many areas of our lives. Do we do this with grace and ease, knowing that all is perfect, divinely orchestrated, and that we are supported, cared for, and loved? Or do we perform this simple act of energy exchange in a way that emanates from fear and ends up feeling graspy and desperate?

It's odd to witness our reaction to our parents, upbringing, and environment, isn't it? We carry so much that's not ours, that isn't true, and is really just part of the collective energy.

I've witnessed myself fall into this state of lack several times in my life. Sometimes it's been self-imposed, other times self-sabotaging, and before yoga, it was just down right unconscious. But the funny thing is this: money is just energy. And energy cannot be created or destroyed. So how could there never *not* be enough? It's just not possible.

But it sure felt possible when I got caught stealing from the company I worked for when I was eighteen. Or the time when I drove my 1984 Mustang to work every day until it literally broke down beyond repair and I couldn't get myself to work. Or when I used the last dollar in my savings account to fly to California on vacation in 1991.

Scarcity felt real when, while pregnant with my second daughter, my then-husband told me that his inheritance was not my money and I had no say in how he spent it. I felt it in my bones when I would say to my children every, single morning, "Hurry up!! We're going to be late!" It was very real when I filed for bankruptcy, lost my business, got divorced, and foreclosed on my home all in one year.

But it *really* became clear that it was a pattern when at forty-four years old, I searched for change in my car, survived on seeds, nuts and protein bars for weeks, and avoided the gaze of homeless people on the streets of San Francisco for fear of the reflection. Yes, at forty-four years old, I finally saw my pattern.

I've spent my entire life recognizing these patterns of lack, falling into them, pulling myself out, falling in and rescuing myself again. Make no mistake as I tell my story here: *I respect where I came from.* I grew up outside Detroit, Michigan in a middle-class family. My parents worked hard and so did my grandparents. But they grew up during the Depression. When my grandmother passed away and we were cleaning out the hall closets, we found about 100 rolls of toilet paper. Apparently she was concerned we would run out!

Her downstairs was converted into a pantry that housed enough canned food for years. In fact, you could live in that pantry, just in case war broke out. She had a full-on secured basement equipped with food, toilet paper, kitchen appliances and a pool table. Oh, and home made wine to boot.

When you or someone in your blood-line has lived through difficult times, there's no question that the survival instinct is in your blood.

THE YEAR I TURNED MY LIFE UPSIDE DOWN

In 2011, I divorced my husband and relocated to San Francisco to start over as a yoga teacher. This wasn't easy as anyone will tell you but I chose not to listen to other people's opinions and set out to start a new life.

I left my children with their father temporarily so that I could get settled. But when I arrived, I quickly realized that it was not going to be as easy as I thought. Rent for a room in Marin County was more expensive than my entire mortgage payment in the Northwest. And food, gas, and utilities were at least 200% more. I was appalled that I had to pay $8 to cross the Golden Gate Bridge every single day. *Every single day!* And, worse yet, this dream job that I moved here for only paid me $4 per student in my class. That sounds glamorous doesn't it? Sure it does—if you have 100 people in your class—but being the new yoga teacher in town, I had no more than two or three people in my classes for at least three months.

I would cry the minute I left that yoga room. Not only was I not making any money, I was *losing* money! I taught at every studio in the area in order to "get my name out there." This meant leaving Marin County early in the morning, heading to the city, then driving over to the East Bay, teaching there, and then driving home. Sometimes I would lead a class with ten people in it, sometimes no one would show up. I went to every single yoga festival to network. It worked to some degree, although unfortunately I gained a reputation for being assertive and pushy, which doesn't always work in an industry that teaches to "flow with the Divine energy of what is."

While I was trying to build a new life for my family, I had also committed to flying back once each month to see my daughters. I took on the role of Art Docent in their school and would fly up on Thursdays and teach 2nd and 4th graders about the Artist of the month. This meant I would miss work, spend about $300 on a flight, plus a rental car, food, gifts, and hotel to keep that connection to my babies. It was heart-wrenching and scary.

I had arrived with what I thought would last me nine months but in less than three months, I was concerned that I wouldn't make it. So I opted out of the living situation I was in and lived out of my car. Yes, that's right—I lived out of my car at forty-four years old.

It always worked out, but the reality was I never knew where I would be sleeping. I showered at the yoga studio almost every day and would take naps in my car in between classes. I never let anyone know how scared I was—I just kept going.

One day, I decided to explore the idea of welfare and food stamps. This was two months before my daughters were supposed to arrive in San Francisco to live with me. I had two months to prove that I was able to take care of them. My back was up against the wall. I walked into the Department of Social Services in San Rafael and took a number. I sat there while every part of my body hurt. My heart was constricted as I looked around the room at the women—yes, all women—waiting in line for support. My heart broke. I could not believe it had come to this.

I knew better. I knew that this didn't have to be. You'd think I would judge these women wouldn't you? Instead, my heart dropped into the deepest compassion you can ever imagine. I wanted to sit there with them and tell them how beautiful they were. I wanted them to know that they had a gift. I wanted them to know that there was a higher power working *for* them. I wanted them to know that they have what it takes to create the life they want. And I wanted them to get up and do it.

And then I realized that this was all a reflection of my own thoughts and beliefs about prosperity. And I wondered what happened in their life that it had come to this. *Why? Why did they not feel worthy of being abundant? Why did I not feel worthy?*

I immediately felt like I was suffocating and dropped into deep fear that I wouldn't get my girls back, and that was enough for me to put my head down and forge forward onto the path of prosperity. I walked out of that office, prayed for every woman in there, and changed my thought pattern. Not only did I change my thought pattern, but I changed the thought patterns for the women in my lineage who came before me and the ones who would come after me—my grandmothers, my mother, and my daughters. This wasn't about me anymore. It was so much deeper.

Two months later, I was teaching at Wanderlust Yoga Festival, had full yoga classes, was leading retreats empowering women, and found a sweet little apartment in Marin County where my daughters and I resided for three years before moving into a bigger house.

I'd watched the reflection of lack show up many times. And then, as if by magic, suddenly I'm living in complete, unimaginable abundance! I do have to admit, though, that when things get really abundant, I can slip back into self-sabotaging behaviors. I've been known to create a story of "loss" because, well, who am I to live in such luxury?

Aha! And there it is! *The worthiness issue.*

This idea of abundance always (and I mean always) comes back to worthiness. How worthy do you think you are? That's the only question that requires an answer.

Very worthy, to answer that question simply.

Who are *you* to receive such beauty, grace and luxury in your life? Who are you? A child of God with infinite resources and unlimited potential, that's who you are!

Your upbringing and ancestral patterns will dictate the way you respond to that question. You most likely instead hear that someone deserves something more than you do. Or that you're just shy of being good enough. I remember distinctly hearing my parents say to me, "Who do you think you are?" and "You should be ashamed of yourself."

Now understand, they didn't say those things to be mean. They were only repeating patterns of lack, limit and self-sabotaging talk from parent to child. They didn't know any better and they really didn't mean it.

I woke up to these patterns inside of myself when I had my own children. It only took one time of hearing these words come out of my mouth for me to start practicing how *not* to speak in terms of lack ever again. I've been conscious to edit my language ever since.

Here's the truth:

> *You are a child of God with infinite resources and unlimited potential. Did anyone ever tell you that? Did they ever tell you that you have the ability to create the life you want just by disciplining your thoughts and emotional state? Maybe when you were really little, if you were lucky. But most likely, if you're reading this book, you have never heard words like that.*

So let me ask you again: How worthy are you to receive such beauty, grace, and luxury in your life?

Just feel into how that question sits in your body for a minute. What happens when I mention the word "worthiness?" Is there a tightening? A constriction? Contraction? What does worthiness feel like in your body? Do you know? Because it's important to note the feeling you get when asked this question.

All the cognitive therapy, spreadsheets, formulas, 12-step programs, affirmations, and mantras cannot solve an embedded illusion of unworthiness. Not one, not ever. It just won't happen.

You have to believe you deserve all the miracles that life has to offer... and then you will be able to receive.

Let me say this: Abundance is not all about money. It's woven into every fiber of your being. It's how you breathe, how you move, how you relate, how you thrive, and it's how you function every day.

Pioneering *your* path to prosperity cannot be boxed into a step-by-step guide. It has to relate to every aspect of your life. You have to believe you deserve the time, the resources, the money, the recognition, and the love... otherwise, it won't happen.

Chanting to Lakshmi—the Hindu Goddess of Abundance—108 times for 40 days won't do it. It will help loosen the stagnation, but your belief system must be reprogrammed from a very deep place in your emotional body.

So I ask you again: How worthy are you to receive such beauty, grace, and luxury in your life?

Look, my parents didn't mean to pass on feelings of unworthiness. They didn't mean to look at life from a survival standpoint. They didn't mean to project their ancestral beliefs of lack and limitation onto me. But it was the deck they were handed and they simply did not have the tools to move beyond that thought pattern.

But I do. So now, I am *pioneering my own path to prosperity.* This does not mean that I am wealthy beyond my fantasies! But I notice the multiple times I fall into lack and I use my tools to bring myself out. I hear my projections of lack and limitation and stop the madness even if I have to correct myself out loud. I observe myself with great compassion and love when I do fall into those old patterns. I say yes without over-burdening myself. I say no when it isn't in alignment with my soul. I notice the constrictions when they show up. I know, in the deepest place in my heart that there is infinite supply and I have access to it—all in one breath.

Pioneering the path to prosperity means that I love myself more than anything on this planet, so when any question of deserving comes up I remember this: It is my birthright to receive all the goodness, joy and abundance life has to offer.

I still sometimes fall into patterns of lack—it's written in my ancestral code. But I needn't inherit those codes. They are my codes to crack and stop the pattern now for my daughters and their children and seven generations after that. It's my work and I gratefully take it on.

I could tell you every story of when I've fallen into lack, limitation, and scarcity. But I don't want to bore you. Every story is the same and that story no longer lives in my body so I can't drop into the drama without asking myself, "Why? Again? You want to tell this story again?"

But here's a few things I want to share with you that came out of those stories:

- *Know when it's time for an upgrade to your system.* A feeling of lack will always come up. When it does, think of it as a moment in time when the Universe is asking you to up-level your barometer of deservedness. The Universe is asking you to upgrade how you see yourself, and you have the opportunity to either stay complacent or step into a bit of discomfort while you transition to a higher level of awareness around your truth and purpose.
- *Stay in tune with your body and your reactions 100% of the time.* Notice your breath patterns, your triggers, chronic pain in your body, and anything that throws you off. Why? Because your body tells stories of your state of being in every second. If you can notice how lack or fear shows up in your body and where it shows up, you can stop it dead in its track and replace it with abundant upgrades. This takes focused intention—yoga, meditation, staying accountable, and self-compassion will help speed up this process.
- *Visualize what you want to receive and feel what it feels like to live in that space.* Don't go after it. Don't chase it. Don't grasp to it when you "get" it. Just be in it and allow your breath to integrate that feeling into your cells. You deserve it. Don't question it or say, "I can't believe it's happening!" Of course it's happening. You created it because you know beyond all knowing that you deserve it. Every last bit of love, grace, joy *and* financial abundance—you deserve it all and more.

When you know that you are worthy of every last bit of love, grace, joy *and* financial abundance, you have embodied it. And then, you will know you are on the path to prosperity.

Dana Damara is one California's most powerful yoga teachers and empowerment leaders. She is a mystic, a mother, a teacher of teachers, and an author. She traverses between the mystical realms, and mothering her two teenage girls. She is an activist for balancing the Divine Feminine and Sacred Masculine in a way that is approachable and digestible to people living in the realms of "real life." She is committed to feminine embodiment, self-love, sisterhood, sacred ceremony and ritual, and creating a safe space for evolution.

When she's not leading one of her fiery, Moon Mystic Classes, she may be facilitating a retreat, hosting a Moon Circle, empowering her clients, creating an inseparable tribe with her Embody Truth Teacher Training program, or simply observing her daughters as they navigate their own karmic path.

She believes that the body has many depths. What happens on the outside is simply a reflection of what is going on inside. It's how we wake up to that wisdom and use it that makes this a human experience. Living in our truth will bring us to the liberation of the mind, ultimately guiding us to infinite love. If we want liberation, we must do the work and it is all based on self-inquiry, exploration, and discovery.

"On the mat, my passion is proper alignment, powerful breath and effortless flow. Time on your mat is sacred space where you find more depth, authenticity and integrity in your life," Damara says. She believes that how you show up on your mat can be directly related to how you show up off your mat. "When we begin to integrate this truth and see ourselves with compassionate awareness, we are liberated from any illusion that holds us back from moving out into the world."

Her greatest teachers are her two daughters, her family, Byron Katie, Seane Corn, Louise Hay, Michael Beckwith, Janet Stone, and every student that has ever walked into her class. Learn more at **danadamara.com.**

Vessels of Abundance

BY AURORA FARBER

Here you are...
Pondering the true meaning of
Abundance, prosperity and wealth.

Scattered in the journeys of your life
And the whisperings of your soul
You will find what you seek.

Sometimes we only recognize
What's already here in the
Retelling of the story.

Sometimes we need a metaphor
To find
The deepest truth.

And so I present to you
A golden tray and
Three vessels of abundance,
Three shapes to decipher,
Three signs to show the way.

Pick them up,
Each in turn
And listen to learn how to
Dance in the mystery
Of abundance.

—Princess Flutterbye

Sip the Abundance of Delight

"A dream come true and I am scared...but also
excited. I think how this trip will change me, and
who I'll be when I return. When I arrive in Madrid,
I'll no longer have the sense of security I have here.
It will be confusing and scary, but still...exciting!
Finally I will live those words, that philosophy that
so struck me when it blossomed...I will live in 'the
freedom from certainty.'"

"JOURNEY TO EUROPE" JOURNAL, SEPTEMBER 3, 1989

In my twenties, I had a philosophy that captured the freedom of those years...I lived in "the freedom from certainty." These words and this freedom came from an inner knowing that was in total contrast from the way I was raised. After college and at the threshold of adulthood, I chose to listen to this inner voice, even in the midst of the cacophony of cultural pressure to get a "real job." With a sturdy backpack, a Eurail pass, and my new philosophy, I set off to roam the uncertain path of the unknown.

Two months turned into six years in Europe. Some family and friends thought I was frivolous; others thought I was lucky. All those years of study to simply wander the streets of Europe? I felt courageous. Not only for living such an adventurous life, but for my desire to buck the societal path of "certainty" that would have me go from college to job to family to mortgage to pension to retirement. That was a cocktail of certainty that I could not swallow.

In contrast, my European life was filled with freedom. Freedom from judgment, freedom from weighty responsibility, freedom from my own incessant voice trying to do the "right" thing. Uncertainty was my playground. I could be or do anything I wanted...without expectation, guilt, or reprimand.

In the arms of uncertainty, I was open to new experiences and exotic adventures. I ate almond cookies for breakfast, drank red wine from a long-necked porron, wandered foreign streets with my tattered map, and danced at la discoteca until dawn. I seized the opportunity to travel to many of the places that sang to my soul. I rode gondolas in Venice; walked in wonder at Chartres cathedral; sun bathed naked on the black sand beaches of Santorini; explored the ruins of Ephesus, Turkey; sang in the ancient theater in Epidaurus,Greece; hiked to Masada in Israel; and rode a felucca down the Nile to visit the temples of Isis and the tombs of pharaohs.

The destinations were breathtaking and incredible. And the journeys... exciting, unpredictable, challenging. I traveled with an open mind and heart, deciding in the moment what my next step would be, way-finding my way toward the next adventure by joyfully following the signs.

When not traveling, Madrid became my home, and later Milan. Financially, I lived month to month, often not knowing how I would buy groceries, pay the rent or even where I'd be living. My focus was not in achieving material or financial success but on how to keep living this amazing life. I listened to my inner voice, and something or someone would always show up, offering the next thread to continue weaving the colorful tapestry of my bohemian life. Whether it was a new job, opportunity, apartment, or friend, the Universe provided and there was always enough.

I felt alive and free, my heart so open that I easily fell in love with everything...ideas, languages, places, people. I found new best friends on overnight train rides. I fell in love with men who fell in love with my passion for freedom. One boyfriend called me "una veleta," a weather vane, shifting and pointing in whatever direction that the wind blew. And it was true. For me, the path ahead was ablaze with the promise of adventure and new experiences, and the one behind littered in beautiful memories and broken hearts.

Living in this "freedom from certainty" left plenty of room for doubt. My journals from that time are filled with questions...and the dreams of possibilities. I asked, What is love? What am I going to do with my life? And I'd write lists and lists of my changing plans. Sometimes I would doubt myself and fall prey to the paternal, cultural voice within that said, "Grow up, get a real job, settle down." Then I would awake to another day in a foreign land and feel the joy of dancing in the mystery of unknown possibilities.

My life was like a passionate tango. Beautiful seductive moves. Pauses ripe with anticipation. And suddenly...a quick swirl of delight or a dip of doubt that came out of nowhere. With delight reigning over doubt, I yearned only for the next step in the dance.

Listening to the fluid, internal music of my soul, I danced in this freedom joyously. I danced in confusion and fear, too. And still I danced, finding my own rhythm of delight in all of it...the light and the shadow. Delight became "the light" that came to me, even in moments of doubt and darkness.

In those years, this daily dance of freedom was seductive and intoxicating...like choosing a frivolous martini off the menu before a delicious meal. Any flavor, any combination, anything my heart desired was available in the freedom from certainty. There were no mistakes, no perfect choices...only adventure and the delightful sip of an extraordinary concoction mixed to please my heart's desires.

THE SECOND TREASURE: A CHALICE
Savor the Abundance of Love

"I'm excited to begin this journey...it feels natural—like a continuation of my soul recovery—and familiar, like going to a new place with a feeling of love in my heart. It feels different too. Not knowing what to expect, only expecting warmth and perhaps a light directing me, "us," where we will go. How I love this man! And yet it seems amazing...so little time together and still, I feel he is a part of my soul. I am scared, but my fears retreat and the 'what ifs' are drowned out by the beating of my heart. I only want to look into his eyes and know this is real."

"JOURNEY TO TAIWAN" JOURNAL, MARCH 4, 1998

After six years of dancing in delight, I longed for a deeper connection, something more substantial, solid, and rooted. I left Europe for the United States and landed a job as a mortgage loan officer.

In less than two years, I was on the societal "path of prosperity." I bought a red convertible and a condo near the ocean. On the edge of the coveted "six-figure salary" and the perfect job to build wealth as a real estate investor,

I once again heard my inner voice calling for adventure and left it all for a different kind of wealth...the richness and magic of love.

I met Rhett in a bar in my hometown while he was visiting from Taiwan. We fell in love in eight days and were married nine months later. Our long distance relationship was held together by words, spoken by phone or written by email, and a deep soul resonance. While apart, we participated in a marriage group (he, in person, me, through emailed notes and homework) and created a Marriage Document of our beliefs and plans for our future. I visited him in Taipei, and we met in Europe and California during our engagement. By the time we were married, we had only spent fifty days together in person.

Our marriage sermon, "Prince Pu and Princess Flutterbye's Search for Happily Ever After," captured the spirit of our union and the two avatars we had chosen to immortalize our love while wandering through the mountains of Taipei. Rhett became "Prince Pu," an ancient, practical, and worldly dragon of the earth, and I named myself "Princess Flutterbye," a butterfly from the celestial heavens, greeting others with a flourish, a bow, and the words "At your service."

These characters were birthed from our love by tapping into our own essence and allowing our magical and mythical selves to emerge. We began to create magical stories of our three favorite things: life, love, and adventure. And our life mirrored our fairy tale stories as we traveled on real world adventures. Together, we climbed the Great Wall, trekked the Himalayas, rode gondolas in Venice, strolled the banks of the Danube in Budapest, marveled at the Coliseum in Rome, and soaked in hot springs near Prague. We spent four months backpacking through Asia, sleeping above pigs and chickens with the Hill tribes of Thailand, roaming the ancient temples of Angor Wat, and gazing at the stars from Tiger Leaping Gorge in China. We also explored adventures of the heart, and became Relationship Educators, teaching workshops in Malaysia, Taiwan, and Hong Kong as we traveled.

After five years together, we decided to start a family. Thrilled to be a mother, I never imagined how much it would change me or how I would forget my mythic essence, the adventurous and daring Princess Flutterbye within. Her ideas of "the freedom from certainty" had no place in my new role as a mother. Instead, I clung to certainty, safety, and security. I worried about the kids when they were sick or unhappy. I wondered whether I was parenting "right." With so much focus on the children, I forgot about nurturing my own needs and the needs of my marriage.

Seven years into our marriage, we moved to Shanghai, China. Rhett focused on his work; I focused on our children. Slowly the wall between us began to solidify until we were more like roommates than partners...our magical union ignored, our mythical selves forgotten. Feeling broken, empty, and alone, I asked for a divorce.

Shocked and heartbroken, Rhett begged me to reconsider. My heart, a steel vault, was impenetrable, until one day, I saw him watching the kids playing in the grass. Our son, mesmerized by a blade of grass, showed his dad this tiny miracle. As tears flooded Rhett's eyes, he whispered, "I can't believe I've been missing *these moments* all these years." Those tears were a healing balm for both of us...opening his heart to presence, opening mine to compassion, forgiveness, and love.

We decided to rebuild our relationship, but this time not only on skills but on values. We realized that knowing relationship skills did not help if we forgot to consciously create our relationship *daily*. With our children as our inspiration, we discovered our family values and created a solid family identity and mission with new rituals and traditions to help us stay on track with our new family vision.

We have yet to discover our "happily ever after." Instead we live moment to moment, sometimes finding challenge, sometimes joy. At each moment we dance in the darkness of uncertainty *together*, each judgment or projection a mirror reflecting back our hunger for love, each trial an opportunity to choose to be like a beautiful lotus and rise from the muck. In those moments we know that the true richness of relationships is the ability to turn our shadows into light, to alchemize the baseness of life into the precious gold of love.

Our marriage teaches me to find the light of love even in the darkness and then to be vigilant about savoring love daily. Love is like a fine wine held in a golden chalice. An abundance of love is always waiting to be poured. We only need to polish the goblet and remember to savor the wine.

THE THIRD TREASURE: A CHAMPAGNE FLUTE
Toast the Abundance of Possibility

"On my way to Hawaii! This has truly been a year
of way-finding. So many wonderful things have
happened since I set sail on the sea of trust and
surrender. Now I cross one sea for another...without
preparation. I'm going to arrive IMPERFECT and
without EXPECTATION. I travel with my heart open
and with the essence of Princess Flutterbye—the
me who trusts, and feels safe in the world, that
loves the mystery and is in communion with life."

"JOURNEY TO HAWAII" JOURNAL, APRIL 5, 2017

My latest journey has been exploring my own internal terrain. As part of a year-long program and initiation into the Divine Feminine, I embarked on a journey to deepen my relationship with my mythic self in order to birth my sacred purpose and work in the world.

During this homecoming, I reclaimed my mythic essence, the one who whispered words of freedom and adventure to me in my twenties; the one who found her name, Princess Flutterbye in sacred marriage; the one I've been dancing with for years, as I forget and re-member her again and again.

And still She comes, shaking up all the ways I still try to carve out security through rules, structure, and the cultural voices of the way things "should" be. Always "at my service," She breaks the chains of control, perfectionism, and not-enoughness that stop me from finally claiming the life I desire. The "She" in me has always known what to do and how to still choose love, despite fear, pain, and confusion.

With Her, doubts become dreams, and so in a sacred circle of sisterhood, I dared to claim Her again. Dressed in turquoise and butterfly wings on my back, I jumped up and down in delight, as I celebrated dreams of the future: to create a successful, sacred business empowering women to ignite their feminine fire and heal the world with love; to travel the United States by RV with my family; to have a house near the beach.

As I boldly embodied my essence, some of those dreams quickly became reality. Infused with Her spirit, we took that amazing RV trip just a few months later. During that journey, I transmuted the false belief that traveling with "freedom from certainty" was possible only when I was young, free, and without children. We traveled like I did in my twenties, waking up to delight, following the signs, and ending the day in a new unplanned, undiscovered place...but as a *family*.

Some of my dreams are still in progress. I'm learning to claim more of my essence than my ego, as I raise a glass and toast the possibility of what is not here yet but of what's to come. Sometimes I hold the glass with confidence, remembering all the signs that guide me. Sometimes I hold it with courage, even in the face of the unknowable path. And sometimes I hold the glass with trepidation and doubt, my smaller, safe self wondering, "Will this actually happen? Am I enough to make my dreams come true? Will this love last?"

My glass becomes heavy with fear and expectation. My body contracts as I shrink away from my soul's divine purpose. And that's when I need to hear Her most, my mythic essence: Princess Flutterbye, whose love of life, love, and adventure have always guided me to live "the freedom from certainty".

At those moments, I hear Her clearly. Her voice no longer a whisper...

My darling, put the glass down.
That's not the way to toast!

Let go of the hesitation, the speculation, and doubt.
And then pick up the glass.

A true toast is seeing what you desire
As already here...

"To your wonderful life
To your amazing marriage
To your happy family
To your good health
To your sacred and successful business
To your financial freedom
To a peaceful planet
To setting the world on fire with love."

See it already here, beloved
And then...

A clink
A swallow
And it is done.
It. Is. Done.

EPILOGUE

It's taken me years to consciously claim my mythic essence daily. The journals and journeys of my life are a testimony of the path we have shared; this chapter, a re-commitment to remembering myself as mythic. I began this writing project in emptiness, having no clue on what to write. Sitting in silence I listened and received the images of three glasses on a golden tray: a martini glass; a chalice; and a champagne flute. With no idea what they meant, I trusted the enigmatic symbols and followed the lead of my mythic essence as she danced my story through these written words.

Now I claim her forevermore. Her spirit...mine. Her rhythm, now matched as we dance in the "freedom from certainty" together. Her gifts, my own to claim and share. Her voice, my voice melting into one, heralding in a new myth of what it means to live in abundance.

So now, dear one,
You've discovered
The secret of abundance is within.

Your stories shape you
Into the magnificent being
You become.
Each day
You write your own myth
Through the choices you make.

So choose to
Shape yourself into a mythic vessel
And catch
Abundance as it pours.

True abundance is not outside you;
It's ever present, all around
In the whispers of your mythic essence.

Will you choose to
Sip delight?
Savor love?
Toast possibility?

The choice is yours, my love...
You are a vessel
Of mythic abundance.

Aurora Anurca Farber, Transformational Coach, Writer, International Speaker and Relationship Educator, is on a mission to help women ignite their "Feminine Fire" (the heart-light within that integrates life-giving power, compassionate love and intuitive wisdom) and believes that these three feminine flames are the key to catalyzing passionate and purposeful action that will heal our world.

She believes that every woman is a sacred vessel, and through integrating our three feminine power centers of womb, heart and mind, we become portals of unlimited creation...whether that is creating a child in the womb, an inspiring business, or a thriving community!

Through private coaching, online programs, women circles and retreats, Aurora creates "sacred spaces" for women to be held, witnessed and loved exactly as they are right here, right now. Her guiding vision is a world of women claiming their creative powers, loving their body temples, and being beacons of fierce wisdom as they burn away archaic, limiting beliefs and set the world on fire with love. Learn more at **aurorafarber.com.**

Special Gift

Visit **AuroraFarber.com/gift** to receive your free audio meditation: "Discover Your Mythic Essence & Create A Life of Abundance".

Spirituality and Money: One Love

BY NICOLE HEMMER

The holy and beautiful devotion to the sacred currency [current] of money.

Money isn't often discussed in the context of spirituality.
What *is* money?

MONEY IS ENERGY.
MONEY IS LOVE.
MONEY IS HONEY.

With money, you can expand and open your life. Money is a tool for soul expansion, growth, and evolution. Money gives you freedom—to be able to have, be, and do what you need to do in this lifetime to support you in becoming what you need to become.

All these negative conditionings around money really need to be burned up. Money is neither good nor bad; it is neutral. It simply is what it is, without any pretenses. It's a tool, one that can feel like a magical wand that can open doors and possibilities, that makes life more magical, alive and colorful. It has the capacity to richen one's life and bring in more dimensions and realms of experiences. Money is a tool that opens gates and portals into previously unknown worlds and realities.

What I see, again and again, is how so many people, especially women, limit themselves "because of money." They become controlled by money. And when you are controlled by money, you aren't free. Anything that binds you, inhibits you, and therefore you are living in an invisible cage. Most people live their lives trapped in the cage of lack, fear and self-imposed suppression because they think they can't afford certain things. They think they can't do certain things, because of the infamous excuse "I don't have enough money," "I can't afford it" or "It's too much." These are self-defeating and untrue statements. And they're part of a heavily ingrained victim conscious-ness pervading us all, as if we are *not* highly powerful Divine Beings capable of embracing the flow of money and thriving in abundance.

When I was fifteen years old, starting out on my path in life, I made a promise to myself that I would never allow the prism of money to stop me from having, being, doing, or becoming the woman I'm meant to be in this lifetime. I would not, I declared, live in a cage.

I am here to live in freedom. I will not be a slave to money. I will not be a victim to circumstances. I will not give away my power to money, as an excuse for not being able to do something I would love to do.

I made a fierce commitment to myself that I will always do what I love and will never be limited because of money. I will always have more than enough money to travel anywhere in the world where I need to go. I will always have more than enough money to invest in my spiritual growth and evolution. I will always have more than enough money to live a beautiful life that's set aflame with my deepest passions and soul congruence.

I am committed to thriving and flourishing in all aspects of my being, and I choose to have money in order to be generous and give. Why? Because it feels so good to give! I give my time, energy, and love in many ways. I also love to give, share, and circulate the flow of money. Money is a river that flows like the streams in the world. The ocean is abundance, and the currents of money all come and go from the ocean of life.

I will always live free, be free, and blaze in the fires of freedom, sim-ply because I would rather die than live as a slave. And if you don't have money to live fully free, you are in someway enslaved. Not only enslaved, but also restricted and limited in your options. I am on this Earth to live: fully, completely, and totally. *Unboundedly*. Wholeheartedly! And I refuse to be controlled by money. Instead, I choose money to be a liberator...a lover...a partner in this co-creation.

You and I are not here to play small.
You and I are not here to shrink.
You and I are not here to live in fear, nor to wallow in self-pity.
We are not here to be dis-empowered.
We are not victims.

Money has given me so much. It's a tool that has allowed me to meet soul family around the world who I would never have had the chance to meet had I not had money as a way for me to travel. It has allowed me to grow in so many ways as I've invested in my education and spiritual development. It has allowed me to live with ease of being, where I can relax and feel ease in my finances. Money has allowed me to experience so much beauty on this Earth through having the opportunity to go to breathtaking sacred sites that are powerful energetic activation centers.

Frederick Lenz, Ph.D, was a spiritual teacher who taught American Buddhism that included the teachings of Tibetan Buddhism, Zen, Vedanta, and Mysticism. He said that many of the highest vibratory places on the Earth are domains of the rich, where certain neighborhoods have more power and some live in these places to use this power to advance one's awareness field. When you have money, you can choose to live in places that hold a high degree of power, which also accelerates your spiritual growth and evolution. I have found for myself that spending time in Hawaii, for example, nourishes and expands my awareness field, whereas spending time in a populated city tends to dull and contract my field.

Money is a source of power because it gives you the power to do what you choose.

When you have money, you have power to makes changes in the world. Perhaps, big changes that affect millions of people, depending on the amount of money you have. When you have money, you can create new structures and implement changes in society that are more in alignment with heart, soul, and spirit. In contrast, when you can barely afford to support yourself, how can you have the time, energy, and resources to serve something greater than yourself?

Worrying about money consumes a tremendous amount of energy. Imagine what you could do with all that energy and time if it were directed toward something that serves the greater good.

Cultivating a strong energetic chalice for receiving, growing, and sustaining wealth and abundance is essential in blossoming in this physical world. If your wealth chalice is chipped or broken, you will not be able to hold this energy (as money is energy!). You'll need to heal and nourish first.

A deep root of what blocks many people from having money is the fear of being powerful (that, and a deeply ingrained unworthiness conditioning). There is a strongly ingrained outlook that money is fundamentally bad, because of those throughout history who have had power and wealth and have not always used that wealth for the benefit of society. Yet, there are those on this Earth now who have money, are deeply rooted in their heart and soul, and are here to create global changes and transformations. I have met them. They use money as a form of power for the benefit of all beings. Their wealth is a tool to create changes in the world, uplift consciousness, and restructure the human paradigm. Bless these beautiful beings who are the trailblazers of the new paradigm of "spiritual people." Spiritual people who have money, wealth, and abundance. It's so needed! It's so required. It's time.

I have friends who are millionaires, friends who have no money, and everything in between. There is also a deeply conditioned outlook in the human psyche that those with money are "bad," "greedy," "selfish," or "not spiritual." We make so many judgments when it comes to money. Truly, the world is in need of spiritual billionaires, conscious beings using the tool of money for the restructuring of this Earth, one that's in sync with the heart and the Earth.

Can you imagine a world where those in power are enlightened beings, who possess a great degree of wealth and know how to use it for the greater evolution of humanity and the Earth? Can we allow ourselves to envision the beauty and possibility of spiritual people thriving in all facets of life, including financially? Why is the financial component of living deemed any less of value and importance than the physical, emotional, and spiritual realms? The perceived dichotomy of money and spirituality needs to be dispelled. We must realize that with money comes power and the capacity to create changes on a global scale of transformation—which is very much needed today. Consciousness brings transformation, yet imagine consciousness and money dancing together.

In my own experience, I have seen that those with money *do* live much freer lives. There is a frequency of ease, support, and wellness that emanates in their presence. It's an emanation of ease, trust, and flow. Money doesn't make anyone more happy, but it does give one much more ample freedom to live in ease in this physical material world. Remember Maslow's hierarchy of needs? Without enough money, we tend to get stuck worrying about physical needs, safety, and belonging rather than progressing up through altruism, self-actualization, and self-transcendence. Struggling to survive isn't healthy or admirable and it's certainly not spiritual. Let's not glorify poverty.

There's nothing spiritual about being broke.

There is nothing enlightening about struggling and *just having enough*. If you look around, you see this Earth and all the multitudes of creation. This life is not just "enough"' it's a overflowing source of abundance in all forms. It's ever expanding, creating, and generating new life every single moment.

Do you think you are separate from the source of life? When you connect with your true nature, you know you are one with life. You realize that money is not separate from you, because, in essence, it *is* you. Money is energy. You, too, are a sparkle of energy. There is an intrinsic union in recognizing the illusion of separation and the falsity of lack, the biggest lie permeating our collective consciousness.

Money is a blessing that allows you to be generous and give from a state of plenitude and fullness. Money can be an offering of love, devotion, and service. With our giving, we can uplift those around us, create change, and crystallize the world with true beauty through embodying and mastering all that we are.

Do you remember how good it feels to give and be generous? It feels so good and uplifting! Why? Because this is our natural state. We are meant to be generous, not constricted, fearful, and selfish.

It's so important to always follow your heart, resonance, and highest excitement. This is the path of beauty, ease, and grace. The way most people operate and live in the world is like this: "I don't have money, therefore I can't do this." AND BOOM. They cut themselves down, without even knowing they are the ones that are limiting their reality. Trapping themselves. How do you know that you are trapping yourself? It doesn't feel good when you trap yourself and say no to following your heart and what you truly desire. In fact, it feels terrible.

It's never that you *can't* do something; rather it's how deeply committed you are to having what you want, or doing what you desire. It's always a matter of priority and commitment.

The basic premise is to trust. Not just lukewarm trust, but divine unfaltering fearless faith. To live in the arms of trust, to awaken to holy grace and know with complete conviction that when you commit to following your heart you will be provided for and supported.

Life and the Universe opens doors for those brave enough to overcome doubt. The doors will always remain closed for those who live in fear. But for those souls that have the tenacity to move outside the cage, and show life fearless faith—they will always be divinely supported. I have lived this.

Be brave. Trust, and always follow your heart and deepest soul resonance. Eternity smiles, and infinity sings.

Nicole Hemmer, MA is a Sacred Feminine Teacher, Inspirational Speaker, Spiritual Guide, Certified Transformational Life Coach and Writer. She leads international workshops, circles and retreats with hundreds of women around the world. Nicole traveled to fifty countries by the time she was twenty-five years old, and has lived in North America, Europe and Asia. She holds a Master's degree in Transpersonal Psychology and passionately inspires women to step into their power and be fully expressed. Nicole initiates, awakens and activates the Divine essence within, and supports women in reconnecting to their Higher Self and Soul Purpose.

As a Modern-Day Priestess, she guides women back to their true nature, self gnosis and illumination. Her signature global mentorship program is her Divine Feminine Soul Leadership program—a three-month immersion for women who are ready to reclaim and live their full feminine power, expression and soulful leadership in the world. Nicole lives globally between Canada, Germany and Bali throughout the year—and will be publishing her first book of Divine Reminders and inspiration for Women of Light with Flower of Life Press in the fall of 2018.

Special Gift

Visit **www.nicolehemmer.com** to receive Nicole's FREE Soul Inspiration Series. Within the Soul Inspiration series, Nicole shares inspiring examples, practices, tools and experiences connected to living a life in unlimited abundance, and mastering the jewels of our soul's journey through thriving and true inner fulfillment.

The Journey to Abundance

BY CRISTINA LASKAR

What does abundance mean to you?

What a question...
Where does one start?
And, as I sit and contemplate this, I know that the answer may be drastically different for most people.

Is it money?
What we've accomplished?
The friends in our lives?
The time spent doing what we love?
Is it following our purpose?
Is it a feeling of worthiness or wholeness?
Maybe it's snuggling a cute fuzzy creature?
Maybe it's a bit of all of it...

Abundance may also mean having enough money to do what we want. But, what if it goes deeper than that? What if we need to *feel* abundant and actually hold the energy of abundance inside of us first?

By reading this book, my wish is that you find your way amongst the many stories to feel what abundance feels like. Because the time is now! It's imperative that our world shift into abundance to alchemize scarcity and the feeling of lack with which we have been imprinted. This is so necessary for us to be able to open up to more love. And, let's face it. Our "lack" mentality is creating much of the chaos that we are witnessing in our world today: wars, competition, corporate ownership of just about everything including seeds, people living in disillusion, the way we treat this beautiful planet as if it's here for our taking...and on and on. Being in scarcity can definitely send us down the rabbit hole of pain and suffering And, yet, we have so much to be grateful for! So, where and how do we focus our energy?

Over the last few years, abundance for me has become a feeling of being rich from within. This requires a deep level of trust in the Universe that there is plenty to go around. For me, abundance is also having great friends and real purpose and passion for what I'm doing. When I feel abundant, I feel *so* alive and inspired, and I enjoy that beautiful connection with others where life is vibrating fully through me, with me, and out of me.

But if this is what abundance is, why doesn't everyone have all their needs met? Why are so many people struggling? I believe much of it is about inequality, lack mindset and our general inability to crack outside of our own conditioning, fear, and unworthiness.

Here's something interesting: The United Nations uses a formula called the *Gini coefficient* to measure the level of inequality that, over time, leads to revolution. The highest level ever recorded on a scale of 0 to 1 before revolt was 0.59 in the Old World in Rome. Can you guess how we rate with inequality here in the United States? Are you ready for it?! We have a score of 0.81! This is crazy...We're supposed to be one of the richest countries in the world. Why is it that we're okay with this huge level of inequality? Especially when the group that has the most money is so small?

I believe that collectively as people we are moving in the right direction towards a shift from a lack mindset to one of abundance. And I know it may seem strange to say this when there are millions of refugees fleeing their country and the homeless population in our own country has skyrocketed in the past decade—and that's barely scraping the surface of all that's going on! I also believe that we must first do the work to tap into the energy and flow of abundance in our own lives so that we can then give back and be in service to All of Life. Once we have a certain number of people living and thriving in an abundance mindset, this will take us to the tipping point to where it becomes the norm for many. And, by tapping into this energy, we find that our own flow and balance becomes easier.

If you are anything like me, balance has not been an easy virtue to stand in. Sometimes the pendulum swing I experience is quite extreme, from working too much and too hard...to burnout and hardly working...and back again. Definitely not sustainable!

When Jane (my amazing friend and publisher) asked me to write a chapter for this book on prosperity—which is seriously edge pushing for *this* lady—I really started to think about the times I had money and the times I didn't have enough. I seem to have been able to maintain an abundant mindset most of the time. Even when I lived out of my van for months, I never felt as if I didn't have enough...(Okay, maybe a few times, like when I was super sick. But I feel as though I can feel that way even now while living in a home when I'm sick. But, I digress...)

So, as we were doing our writing planning and focus session (which is like an energy healing/therapy session, because, yeah, Jane is that good), we dove into who I am, how I'm wired, what worked for me as I was growing up, and my beliefs around prosperity and abundance.

I'll share a little snippet as to how I'm wired so by using me as a mirror, you can perhaps understand yourself and/or those you love a little better. I am loud, bossy, fierce, sweet, tender, rebellious, and highly emotional (I am always working on emotional intelligence, and boy oh boy is it edge pushing and requires a lot of quiet processing). I am protective of those I love, and I have a crazy affinity for honesty, justice, and equality. I am a warrior spirit.

One of the things that drives me is *purpose*. Humans, as opposed to our animal brothers and sisters on this planet, need a purpose, especially those high-energy warrior spirit folks. More accurately, we need to *know* that we have a purpose. We're not satisfied with simply *being* and *doing*. When we don't have a purpose, we feel lost; and when we feel lost, we tend to find trouble. (This is coming from a mother of a child who is very similar to me.) We love efficiency and typically have an abundance of energy. We're often misunderstood and not always liked. We can seem serious and distant, due to our active brains. And, then when you are the focus of our attention, it can feel like a lot. If you are able to hold the energy of people like this, you can receive the gift in its power—it's amazing! I bet you know some people like this.

As a child, I had lots of energy! I was walking (practically running) by seven months. My mother shared my walking story a few years ago when I was starting a large business endeavor: from Ayurveda Practitioner to founder and CEO of a crowd-funding/crowd-sourcing social networking platform based around vetted nonprofits.

She said, "Oh, Cristy, why don't you start out a little smaller?! It's not as though you came into this life running."

"Oh Mom, will you tell me my learning how to walk story?"

"Sure. I'll never forget it. You were seven months old. We were at your 2nd cousins house and she had twins the same age as you. Her twins are both being propped up sitting on the couch watching television. You were practically running around their coffee table holding on with one finger as you chanted 'shit, shit, shit' like the train rhythm. It was so embarrassing."

"I was seven months old?"

"Yes, you were. You started most things early…"

"Seven months old and practically running when most kids are starting to crawl. It sounds as though I came into this world running…"

"Oh Cristy, that's not fair. How did you get me to validate your story like that?! I can't believe you just did that to me."

And, then we both had quite a good laugh, and still do today about this story!

As a child, I did not like dresses (and I was my mother's first child). She often says, "Oh, Cristy, I just wanted to dress you up in all of the cute outfits. And, every single time, without fail, first thing you would do is go and sit in a mud puddle." Yup, that was me: rebellious and way too active to try and figure out how to do the dress thing or, for that matter, the girl thing.

I would much rather have been in the woods. I would always disappear outside and run all over the neighborhood. I knew where I wanted to go and/or what animals I wanted to see. The neighbors would actually call my mom to give her a "Cristy sighting". We had a decent-sized forest in our backyard plus animals (dogs, horses, and rabbits) and a trampoline. So, when I needed to escape, I would hang out there. (I mean sitting in the house and just playing with toys was so BORING!) I was actually grounded by my parents for the first time at the age of four because I didn't come home after dark. In my defense, it was winter. So the daylight hours finished way sooner than I could fathom.

My grandparents had a very nice farm that we spent a lot of time. And, being the high-energy, driven person that I am, I was totally content to wake up before most of my cousins or siblings and go help shovel cow shit. I absolutely loved this! I got to be around animals, and I was doing something that was of use to others. Granted, I loved to feed the animals a lot more, since

I got to look them in the eyes, but still, shoveling shit was also fun to me! It gave me a sense of purpose. I mattered. I was of value. That feeling was, and still is, priceless. Interestingly, no one would congratulate me for going to work; it was just what had to be done. As a reward, my Uncle Phil would sometimes squirt me with fresh milk straight from the cow's teats. I'd scream from shock, but I loved it.

I tell you all of this because of the sense of purpose and what it does for us as humans, some of us more than others. Some of us are more trusting; we simply know that we are going to be living our purpose with whatever it may be. Some are more comfortable simply being. We all have different flavors of how we walk through life and what purpose means to us. None are better than anyone else's. It's just are the way we operate.

About ten years ago, I heard that an indigenous culture in South America believes that if a child does not have a purpose by the age of three, they will walk through life a bit lost. This particular tribe sends their three-year-old with their older brother to go fish on the Amazon river. This got me thinking about our culture and how we baby our children. So many questions came flooding in! Is this why we see so many kids with entitlement issues? Is this why, even at such a high level of upset throughout our country, there has not been a more major, unifying revolution?

PTSD is such a massive problem these days for soldiers returning from war. But, there have always been wars. So why are so many of our soldiers coming home today with PTSD? I believe it comes back to lack of purpose and lack of belief in the cause. I once heard an interesting distinction between soldiers and warriors: Soldiers are those who fight battles for other people—they may or may not believe in the cause; warriors are those who fight for what they *believe* in. PTSD was less of an issue amongst warriors, because they had purpose; they believed in the battles they were fighting.

Having a purpose plays an important role in our psychological health. This is true for some people more than others. A purpose can be anything, really—it doesn't just have to be a grandiose endeavor! One can find purpose in raising children or caring for animals. Purpose can be found in cooking or in decorating your home. One's purpose can be small acts of random kindness, or it can be practicing patience or facing whatever challenge you're choosing to work on. In this sense, purpose is a lot like presence.

FUN WITH PARADOXES

Have you ever experienced how one truth could be totally true while the opposite is true, as well?

For me, abundance is the result of finding balance inside the paradox by identifying the third option in the center, such as the balance of being present AND living my purpose, or the balance of allowing my intense feelings while also recognizing my own learned conditioning. It's about coming into alignment with the truth, and letting go of the extreme black or white thinking that is so pervasive in our culture and so easy to slip into. Abundance is finding the balance of how we want things to be and with how things *really* are. It's the balance of being with discomfort while having the courage to shift your vibration and redirect your focus—which then brings us back to our purpose! Do you see how these things are completely intertwined? See if you can open your awareness to the countless paradoxes in your life.

And, always, come back to center.

Contemplate the following:

- How do you find the balanced option that is right for you?
- How do you balance your masculine and feminine energies?
- How do you find the balance between *doing* and simply *being*?

These answers are going to be different for each of us. I happen to love therapy as a tool for finding balance and thus bringing myself into a vibration of abundance. It's very empowering as I peel back the layers of conditioning and rewire myself so I can come home to the real me! Meditation is also a fabulous start to the day—or fabulous whenever you can fit it in. Nature is one of the most blessed forms of medicine, which then brings me to movement—do what feels good to you...just do it!

Also, just surrender. I know we hear this word all the time, and it can be a little daunting when you don't know where to start, so start small. Start by setting an intention, doing the work that needs to be done to set that desire in motion, and then watch to see what happens. Maybe there's a different path for you to take. I personally had no idea I'd be starting a tech business when most of my adult life was leading me towards the world of health and wellness (though Connectavid is also leading toward global health).

Abundance is getting to know yourself more and more so you know what's right for you and what isn't. Then, you can be firm in your boundaries while leaving your heart open for love WHILE standing in your truth.

These aren't overnight fix-its—because truly there is no finish line on this path of prosperity! It's about the journey. The journey is why we're here! So enjoy it. Stay true to yourself. Trust. Surrender. Go with flow. Everything's really an adventure, so delight and prosper in the ride!

Cristina Laskar is the founder of Connectavid, a website for connection, collaboration, and contribution to build strong communities around causes. Connectavid is a place for users to confidently share their voice, to strengthen connections, and to impart knowledge. It's the meeting ground for leaders to find help, understanding, and to embrace limitless possibilities. As a facilitator for fully integrated healing,

Cristina was formerly a Wholistic Healthcare Practitioner. She started Connectavid as a way to ask us to remember our true nature and to live accordingly. Her background in Ayurveda and Traditional Chinese Medicine, and certification in Ayurvedic massage and Marma therapy helped chart this path. Cristina's passion for healing led her to create Connectavid in order to have a larger impact that brings lasting change. Connectavid's mission is to inspire awareness, acceptance, and responsibility—to bring about progressive leadership towards an empowered future. Connectavid is passionate about keeping it light, but sincere. Its goal is to find ways to play, interact, and to do something unusual. It's a place to cultivate good listening, with a nod to bettering this planet and its inhabitants for countless generations.

The heart of Connectavid lies in reminding people that we're all in this together and to empower people to take charge. As we find our health, happiness, and limitless love within, we become more aware that we can only make change together.

Cristina is a mother of two teenage boys who inspired her to learn about health and healing. They also gave her a great desire to leave this planet in a better place for them and future generations. Contact Cristina via direct message at **connectavid.com.**

Special Gift

Visit **www.connectavid.com** to create your free profile.
When you do, Cristina will plant a tree for you with Eden
Reforestation Projects!

Abundance as the Gift Evident

BY GRACE LAWRENCE

CHRISTMAS 1965

Presents piled high under the tree, fresh green garlands with red bows gracing mantles, baskets of Christmas cards sharing good tidings from friends and family, carols playing on the stereo, and mouth-watering fragrances coming from the kitchen. Ours appeared to be a picture-perfect Christmas.

Yet, coming down the stairs on Christmas morning the year I was fifteen—old enough to have long ago cast Santa into the corner of crushed fantasies—I felt the heavy weight of what Christmas day would require and what would be expected of me. I was consumed by a familiar mixture of hope, dread, sadness, and shame.

This heaviness wasn't new. I had felt it even as a seven-year-old. I remember the first time the pure magic facade of Christmas began to crack. Too excited to sleep, my brother and I had slipped out of our beds. In our footed pajamas, we snuck down to the first landing so we could peer around the corner and catch a glimpse of the cheery ho-ho man in the red-and-white suit pulling our presents out of his huge sack.

Instead, we saw our parents on the floor, assembling what would become a puppet theater. I remember thinking that maybe Santa had already come and my parents were simply his helpers. But, hearing them talk in low voices about A tabs and C slots, I realized that something wasn't as I had thought it to be.

Even at seven years old, I knew that my mother wanted our Christmas day to be the best and most perfect for her two children. Our parents were trying to keep everything light and happy. At the same time, I knew they weren't happy. Our mother was living with a husband who didn't love her and was struggling with what we later recognized as mental illness. My father carried deep hurt; the early death of his sister had been followed by a nasty divorce between his parents, shattering an already heartbroken family. My parents were making the best of it within their individual heartaches.

Every Christmas, I wondered what was wrong with me that I couldn't just go along with the giving and receiving of presents, saying thank you and meaning it.

How is it that there has always been this existential distance between the appearance and the felt experience of abundance?

My father had a couple of photography stores and a family inheritance, and my mother carried the post-war distinction of being a "housewife" with an active social life. My brother and I attended private schools. We went on family vacations and had a pond, creek, *and* a pool in the yard, along with gardeners and household help. Our parents hosted and attended cocktail parties, mingling with attorneys, doctors, and brokers and, of course, their housewives.

Just under the surface of this abundance, there was a sense of lack, of bereftness, of disconnectedness. While my family enjoyed a wealth of things, I never felt that any of this was feeding me, touching me, or interacting with me. Rather, it was the backdrop of a lonely isolated existence. The truth was, I felt poor. Maybe we all did.

When my mother was growing up, she actually was poor. Her parents moved with their seven children from the Midwest to California during the Depression. A photo I have of them looks like it could be an illustration for *The Grapes of Wrath*, several pairs of young barefooted legs hanging out the windows of a tired and dusty jalopy. My mother, a brave and enterprising woman, went north to attend Stanford Nursing School, then worked as a pediatric nurse in San Francisco. There she met and married my father, who, while working as a professional photographer, inherited a fortune as descendant of the men who created the Caterpillar tractor.

My mother was outgoing and generous with formidable determination, while my father was naturally cautious and had deep anxiety about the money running out one day. I often wondered if it was safe to believe that we really did "have money." It might *look* like it, but did we really and would it last?

My mother would try to assure me, saying, "Your future is secure." Yet she never told me what this meant, except to imply that I shouldn't worry. But, like my father, I did.

Money was given as a gift, but it was also used as a weapon.

If I was a good girl I was given cash for a shopping trip. But if I misbehaved or otherwise went astray of expectations placed upon me, money would be withheld and shopping trips canceled.

Whether I was deemed deserving or undeserving depended on my mother's mood, which in turn depended on whether she was on a drinking binge and on the attack or if she was sober and feeling great about life. If there was a pattern, I could barely predict it let alone depend on it. Each of us played our part as an isolated character, without a script or any briefing on the contextual story in which we were to play a part as a family touched by alcoholism.

REFUGEE FROM ABUNDANCE

At thirteen, I began rejecting the abundance I grew up with. I wanted to find a way out into the world beyond the confines of the life that seemed to be swallowing me up. My first step was to quit private school and enroll in public school for the first time. This was in 1963, just before our country was about to experience the first of several politically motivated assassinations. Our nation's identity was crumbling around the edges, as was the surety of life's plan that had been set out for me. While it looked like I was following the steps in that plan—high school, college, and then nursing school, marriage, and family—I vowed to do it my way, rejecting what I saw as a world of empty wealth.

As soon as I finished high school I essentially ran away to college with little a sense of what I was up to. While on the surface I rejected notions of wealth, I let my parents pay my way. In college during the late 1960s, I found myself gravitating toward fellow students who questioned the status quo and felt the rising tides of cultural change. By the time I came back home to attend nursing school, I was a different person and our world was different, too. Though I may not have had a clear sense of where I was going, I believed and declared I was never to return to "where I had been."

Over the next decade, I lived in many places, establishing enriching encounters with like-minded people. This was a dynamic period in which I was discovering what I loved—collaborating with colleagues, community with women, and attending to the caring for others. On the other hand, I was wakening to what I would *not* tolerate anymore—no more relationships that didn't uphold truth and trust as guiding principles, and no more trying to fit into others' ideas of what was right for me and my life. Ahead of me laid a move to Canada, another nursing school, a marriage and a divorce, an apprenticeship as a lay midwife, another relationship, a pregnancy, the birth of my son Tam, motherhood and, beneath it all, the search for how to make sense of what all of this was about.

About the time Tam was three, I fell into an exhaustion and was diagnosed with an unspecified hepatitis. As I recovered, I realized that my relationship with Tam's father wasn't working, and it was harming both of us. Leaving, too, felt threatening. But I was presented with the option of cutting my losses and getting out, for the safety and sake of myself and my son. These were some of the most difficult years of my life.

I returned to Palo Alto—near my hometown of Los Altos—to stay with my dearest friend, Betty. "Just for a while," I declared. "Just until I get my feet under me once again." I had been re-inspired by another quest, this time to attend a school of transpersonal psychology in New Mexico. I was on my way and would just be taking a short break. Or so I thought.

SANCTUARY

It started with a cold that proved unresponsive to herbs and potions, accelerated into fever, and eventually required medical intervention. After days with no improvement, I woke to learn that Betty had called my parents and they were on their way to come and take me home: *their* home, which once was my home, the one from which I fled years before.

The last place on earth I wanted to be.

Weak with fever and sustained illness, I had neither the strength nor wherewithal to resist. Even as I saw my mother standing at the doorway of my friend's home and cowered against the door frame, pleading silently against the inevitable, I had but one choice—to allow my parents to care for me and to surrender to sleep and healing.

I don't remember very much of the weeks that followed, except for my father coming to my bedside from time to time to give me my medicines and tend to the fresh narcissus my mother would pick for me by the creek. As I recovered, it became clear to me that I needed to return to Canada to bring things to a close. My failed relationship required attention and proper severance: Property needed to be sold, possessions given away or packed for shipping, and farewells uttered.

While in Canada at a party at a friend's house, I received a phone call from my mother. She had found a house. "It is perfect for you," she said.

She and my father would buy it for me, but I would have to make a decision in the next twenty-four hours—sight unseen—as I was in Canada and the house was in California. Was this as an act of love or one of control in the name of love? Was I really going to live near my parents again? I said yes.

The little house *was* perfect for Tam and I, and we loved it. It was a bungalow, with an enclosed garden and situated in a safe and quiet neighborhood. Thus began a new chapter in our lives. I was a single mother with a home of my own and Tam was happy. I was working at things I enjoyed, and I was putting down roots.

As it has always been with abundance and I, the arrangement had unsettling aspects. Because my parents owned the home, my mother, still suffering from alcoholism and mental illness, decided this gave her the right to breach boundaries, just as she had when I was a child; she would pick the lock to my bedroom door and barge right in. One day, she came to our home drunk and I refused to let her in. She pounded on the front door, tore down the fence gate, and made clear that she was ready and prepared to break the windows if necessary. My body shaking and ice-cold, I called the police, who came and took her to the hospital.

My mother never forgave me. Neither did my father, who described the incident as "what I did" to my mother. What I *did* was to take ownership of my life. Thus, a new ground was being laid into which abundance could plant her seeds, the first of which was through a family friend who offered to guide me through the steps toward financial freedom, eventually leading to full ownership of my home. This was a significant and provident threshold in itself, leading to my subsequent move to Oregon a decade later.

LIFE? OR DEATH?

Time marches on. My parents have died, and my son has his own beautiful life now. Though I am financially comfortable and have a wealth of blessings that can be named, I can't seem to shake that old feeling I had that Christmas long ago that something isn't right, that I don't fit in, that somehow I'm not able to enjoy things the way other people can.

By the time I found my current home a few years ago, I had been struggling with a depression that had been weaving in and out of the years of my life and I knew that this would eventually mean turning my face toward what *really* lay underneath.

In December 2016, on the Winter's Solstice, I went to a retreat where plant medicines would be offered within a protected and ceremonial context. I had declared my intention: to approach the medicine with an earnest request for insight and healing of whatever this depression was about. I felt that I had tried everything I knew and, still, the darkness and the despair persisted.

I had prepared by discontinuing my antidepressant medication months beforehand. All went well the first night. The next day, however, down I went into the rabbit hole of the unexpected where Abundance took me by the hand.

Forty-eight hours later, I open my eyes and see my son. But his words don't make sense. He tells me I'm in the ICU. That I lost consciousness while at the retreat. That I had been dropped off at the hospital. That I'd been there a couple of days.

"What? What did you say?" He tells me again. And once more. I can't quite make sense of it. I close my eyes.

Some time later, my eyes open and see my daughter-in-law, her face close to mine. She looks so lovely. I reach for her and say her name. She takes my hand, close to her cheek. I realize how much I love her, close my eyes, and am gone.

Time passes and again I wake. A young nurse is calmly, confidently moving about the room. She smiles at me, seeing that I have wakened. *Oh my God. Why am I here?* She explains in simple terms. Attempting to attain some semblance of control, I explain that I am a nurse, have worked rehab and hospice. *Oh my God. I am a patient and my body is here in this gown! Unacceptable.* I drift back to sleep.

I wake. Movement, bright lights. I'm being transferred to another unit. I'm disappointed. I liked it where I was. It must be that I am going to live after all. But first, I have to be a patient. A nurse's nightmare. *Oh my God.*

Over the next weeks, I pieced together the circumstances in which I had detoured into a touch-and-go meeting with death. Tam told me that when I arrived at the hospital I was in critical condition. I had been intubated and put on life-support while my body was brought back into balance, which took a couple of days.

Weeks later still, I realized that I had been having an encounter with the deepest parts of myself. While in this timeless place, I was considering taking my leave from this life. *Living* this life was just too hard, I claimed. Yet another aspect of myself knew better and sought counsel. I was then met with the most loving eyes—eyes that knew me through and through, for she was me, in a Higher form. Her words to me were, "You are early, Grace." I had tumbled onto an opportunity to leave this physical life and now I was confronted with what this would mean in the greater scheme of things. Finding myself in unfamiliar territory, I asked "What do I do?"

Thus began a review of the sort we hear about from near-death survivors. Gently coaxed to remember and reflect on the truth that I was about to be reaping the fruits of all the work I had done in this life so far, I realized that I must return. I wanted to finish what I had started. I had family, and I hadn't said goodbye. There were my friends...and my drawers and files that hadn't yet been cleaned. I couldn't "just leave."

Enfolded in a space of uncompromising and unconditional love, I chose to return with a renewed sense of commitment. I *chose* life. I chose life not *over* death, but life interwoven with death. Both ever-present. As one.

The dying are busy in their process of leave-taking. It can look like hours... or days...or minutes...of very little "going on" to those that stand nearby. What we can do for them is to be present with a quiet abiding and allow them the way of their choice-making. This is the greatest gift that we can give. To come alongside and hold the space as sacred, knowing that what is thought to be darkness is actually full of life eternal. It certainly was for me.

THE BUDDHA IS IN THE KITCHEN

While with my family in Seattle for this past Christmas, Tam asked me if I would ever consider revisiting my childhood home. "Absolutely not!" I exclaimed. "There are too many horrible memories there."

He quietly looked at me and said, "There were good things that happened there, too."

That night I dreamed I was in that kitchen. Sitting in a chair was a woman who is a current-day Yogini teacher. When I woke up from the dream, I thought of the teaching: *The Buddha is in the kitchen.*

I remembered that back in those days, in that house, when any of us would ask my mother what she wanted for Christmas or for her birthday, her answer was invariably: "Love and appreciation. That's all I want." It seemed to be phrased as a challenge, and every time I thought to myself, "Damn it! We give that to you all the time! Don't you know? Will it ever be enough for you?"

It took me decades to realize that she *didn't* know and it would *never* be enough. No matter how many times love was expressed or appreciation demonstrated, it couldn't ever be enough. All she could do was reject it and conclude that we—her family—were the reason why she felt unloved and unappreciated. She didn't have the instinct to look within herself.

During the years she was my mother, this was the root of all of our contentious encounters as well as those rare but relished moments when love flowed through and between our hearts. Perhaps the greatest pain of my life was this "unfixable" thing; despite doing and trying everything I knew, including innumerable attempts to offer her the deep love I felt for her and being furious when she couldn't receive it, the impasse between us persisted.

When Tam said to me "There were good times, too," something clicked, and what I had always seen as a frustratingly persistent demand was, in fact, the flip side of my mother's equally and basically good and generous nature. She enjoyed the giving, but when it came to receiving, especially from her family, she couldn't. She doubted. She fought back. And with the cruel counsel of the chemical effects alcohol had on her system, she believed that there wasn't enough love for her. Ever.

My refusal to look back was like erasing all those times when generosity and love of life filled the rooms, when the California breezes felt afresh with the promise of a new day, the many times my brother and I stayed up late to share a little doobie and watch "The Twilight Zone" and "Star Trek" on the black-and-white TV set, or when I had pool parties in the backyard and my parents kept themselves discreetly out of the way.

She passed on to me—and I accepted—the beliefs and inner structures of a generous heart and kind and loving intention. But I also internalized a strong and defiant inner hand that raises itself to block love from freely streaming in. Here and now, seeing my mother in this light and opening my heart to her, I feel in my body the relaxation of forgiveness. *For she knew not what she did.* Nor did I know. Even today, I know not the half of what I do, especially when I refuse love's expressions into my heart, or don't allow abundance to reach deep, deep down into the pockets of pain I hold onto as if life itself were at risk if I were to let it have its way with me.

I am my mother's daughter as she was her mother's daughter and on up the line of our ancestry. Abundance offers a choice at every turn. We choose in every moment. I can choose to continue to suffer and wonder and berate and refuse. Or I can see the gift evident and forgive from the love that freely streams through my heart. That burden that has been passed down and lived through each of our lives can be seen simply as the refusal of love that holds inside it the option to choose love abundant.

Abundance offers a choice at every turn.

Today, some six decades after that Christmas when I saw my parents playing Santa, I feel a relaxation in my being. I realize that this is what forgiveness feels like—a releasing of long-held presumptions, firm declarations, and a refusal to love the other in all their human foible and fullness. My mother was who she was, and I loved her. I love her today. But, looking back, I can feel forgiveness for her in a deeper way, and perhaps that is the true abundance I have been looking for all along.

Abundance isn't just one thing. It is in the awareness of the perfection of everything, that the divine lives in every little bit, in all our stories and experiences, in all of nature's glory, in our own selves, and in every single moment. Each of these is a world unto itself, ready to spill out its gifts, each one a message from the mystery. All we need to do is open and ask to be shown.

Grace Lawrence's deepest quest has always been to discover that One True Thing that exists every-where, in and out of time. For her, this quest is deeply personal and has pulled her forward throughout her life.

Professionally she has worked as an RN in the fields of rehabili-tation and hospice. She has also studied home birth midwifery, death midwifery, Tibetan Bud-dhism and esoteric Christianity as well as botany, landscape design and the science and art of flower essences. More recently, she has turned to writing as her inner allies have come forward to guide and support her.

When not writing, Grace is often in her garden or in the forest, lean-ing against a large tree or lying on the moss. Or, she just might be binge-watching some Netflix.

She is currently delving back into death midwifery and developing coursework on death planning.

Connect with Grace at **gracejlawrence@gmail.com** or at f**acebook. com/grace.lawrence.520.**

Facing My Self

BY AMANDA LEIGH

As I sit here writing, wondering where to begin and where all of this started, I'm brought back to my childhood. Somewhere along the way in the deep recesses of my mind, I developed the premise that I wasn't worthy of receiving abundance or worthy of receiving love. And there's irony, because my name, "Amanda," means worthy of love. Years of being pushed away by people, rejected, not fully accepted for who I am, shutting down the most sensitive and intuitive parts of myself because they were *too intense* for other people, developed the perfect conditions for me to truly believe that no one would ever want me. That I wasn't "good enough" to experience or receive the type of love/relationship I desired and dreamed of. That if I didn't settle and say yes to this one man's proposal, I would be alone.

I was nineteen when I packed up my belongings and drove from Massachusetts to Alaska with Z. There were signs along the way, like his camera equipment being more important than me, a human being; being called terrible names; no expression of love other than sex, which quite frankly wasn't love. I was young and had experienced only one other partner prior to him, so I didn't know what actual love felt like, or what sex as an expression of love felt like. It was just an animalistic need, a duty to perform.

I stayed.

Eventually, Z proposed while we were laying in bed one night. It wasn't an earth-shattering experience. It didn't make me cry like we see in couples who have risen into love with each other. I accepted the proposal out of fear.

Fear of what would happen if I said no.

Fear of how I would get home—a mere 5,000 miles away—or support myself.

Fear that if I turned down this proposal that I would live my life alone and that no other man would ever want me.

Fear that I wasn't good enough and, at the same time, was too much.

I was afraid to leap into the unknown and so I chose, out of fear, to accept far less than my heart desired.

> *When we make choices from fear, we block the flow of abundance—our ability to receive. Abundance and prosperity, while often associated with financial wealth and freedom, are so much more. True abundance and prosperity come from allowing yourself to be open to receiving and experiencing the flow of love, life, connection, natural abundance, and happiness that exists within us and through us.*

Several people asked, over the course of the months we were engaged, whether or not I wanted to marry Z. They were joking in their asking, but underneath the jovial asking was a message I was continually hearing inside of myself...

Do you want this? Do you truly believe that you are not good enough, not worthy of receiving love, not worthy of receiving abundance? Do you believe that I, the Universe, your Goddess-like Self, am not here to support you?! Do you believe the bullshit stories you have been creating for yourself?

I did.

I believed the stories and rational-lies of unworthiness that I repeated to myself. Abundance? This was a foreign concept for me. I didn't believe I was worthy of receiving *anything*.

Each time I was asked whether or not I wanted to marry Z, I would experience a stirring inside of myself. It felt somewhat like fear, but underneath the fear, looking back, was excitement. Excitement of what exists in the unknown. I didn't trust it though, nor did I trust myself. Every single time, I said yes. Every single time, I said yes when the *fiber of my being* was screaming *NO!* I turned my back on myself, on my inner voice, on my intuition, on my higher guidance, on the very core of who I am.

Few wounds go deeper than those caused by choosing to turn my back on myself.

The opportunity exists for us to view feelings of fear as fear, and run away; or to reframe what we perceive as fear into excitement and dive into the unknown. It's when we choose to release feelings of fear, of lack, or limiting beliefs, that we create space (as frightening as it may feel) for more abundance to come into our lives.

I married Z just three weeks before my twenty-second birthday. I sure as hell didn't know who I was let alone what I wanted in life.

The first year of marriage felt like a slap across the face.

There were the little things: Always having to be the one to ask to do things together. Needing to ask for flowers, which always seemed to dampen and spoil the receiving of a gift, not speaking the same love language and not being able to see his way of expressing love. Looking back now, I cannot tell you what his love language was or how he expressed it. Love was a language that Z and I didn't speak. The pain of not knowing how to navigate our relationship via love was excruciating. I struggled to adjust to life in cold Alaska in a cabin with no running water, five thousand miles from anyone else I knew, and he called me names and had disdain for my intense nature.

There were exchanges that continued to emphasize my internal belief that I did not matter. The "good" jobs in Alaska can be challenging to come by unless in the height of tourist season, and that's not when we arrived. Z took a job on the North Slope on the oil fields that winter and was gone every three to four weeks for several months. I had a lot of time on my own during those months and long, dark, cold nights.

All this forced me to begin to reclaim my personal power, and provided me the smallest and slightest glimpse into who I was beneath all the noise. At one point, Z returned home from the Slope and stated that I had changed. Of course I had changed! I began to see what I could do, who I was, what life was like without him—and I felt the shame of even imagining that...

After months away and just before the start of the tourist season, Z expressed an interest in working at Denali National Park again—a three-hour drive from where we were currently residing. We had agreed for him to head down for the interview, and if he were offered a position, for us to discuss as a family whether it was worth us spending another three or four months apart.

Z returned home from the interview and told me he had accepted the position as a bus driver in the park and would be leaving soon.

It felt like another slap across the face.

I knew, without a doubt, that I did not matter, not in the least. In the grand scheme of things, I was ranked somewhere on the bottom of priorities. And I was pregnant with our first son.

I spent the summer alone in the cabin with our two dogs, and worked at the airport. What little connection Z and I had was more or less gone. Shortly after our son was born, we moved again. It was still winter, I was nursing, and now felt more isolated and alone than ever. I was grateful for hot running water, a flush toilet, and a dishwasher. Of course, no convenience could fulfill the hole that was growing inside of my heart.

I became despondent and much like a wallflower, only less flower-like, and more like a part of the wall. My light, my shine, my sparkle, had dwindled down to a mere ember of its potential. I remember one time Z had a friend visit and they had decided to go out looking at the wildlife one day. It was his friend who said, "Aren't you going to invite Amanda?"

I felt invisible. My sense of worth was dying. And still, I stayed.

Finally, after more than three years of not having seen family, we moved back to Massachusetts.

It was then that I began to truly see.

I began to see how I needed to allow myself to be put down in order to be in relationship with Z. I began to see how I was not being allowed to communicate or express my feelings. It was then, in the home of my grandmother, Goddess rest her dear and loving soul, that I began to see how I had been hiding myself—the blessed, beautiful, emotive, flowing, feminine evolutionary parts of myself—in order to feel accepted and understood by my family.

Looking back now, it hurts.

It's painful seeing, hearing, and feeling how I have dimmed my light over the years. How blocking myself—a beautiful misunderstood intuitive, hypersensitive empath—blocked my ability to receive and experience the bounty of abundance surrounding me. To receive and experience abundance, I know, it's vitally important to act in alignment with who we truly are.

We moved into an apartment. Our relationship really began tanking, but I was also pregnant with our second son. I remember my OB/GYN asking early on if I was happy about the pregnancy. There was a part of me that was…and there was a part of me that wasn't happy being pregnant, that wasn't happy carrying this man's child, that wasn't happy by any means whatsoever being in relationship with Z.

Even after becoming pregnant with our second child, I didn't leave. Maybe it was not having a model of a healthy a marriage or relationship. Maybe there was a part of me that believed suffering was a necessary part of being married.

After I gave birth for the second time, Z quickly returned to work.

The pain continued. I was alone.

I allowed myself to experience a form of not only emotional & verbal abuse but sexual abuse when he would come home late at night looking to have his "needs" met. I would inevitably submit.

I lay there like a fish. Dead. Cold. Unresponsive. Disconnected. Dissociated.

I had given up all of my sovereignty in order to maintain what little sanity I had and get what little sleep I could.

Eventually, I sought out counseling, convinced that there was definitely something wrong with me. I was worried for myself and for my children. It was during that time that I realized that the majority of what I was feeling and experiencing were due to the relationship I was in. I tried to make the marriage work, but a successful relationship would require both of us to show up. Z wasn't willing to show up. He wasn't willing to meet me halfway.

There was one afternoon or evening we'd had another argument. I locked myself in our bedroom and noticed a bottle of Tylenol sitting on the bureau. Placing the bottle of Tylenol in my hand, I sat on the bed and contemplated suicide.

Is this all there is to life?
Am I meant to live a life of suffering?
Am I meant to spend my life miserable and unhappy?
What would happen if I took a bunch of Tylenol? I could do it. I could choose to check out. If I did that, I wouldn't have to suffer anymore, I could finally be free.

What about the boys, though? Who would take care of them? I don't want him raising them...

Would it be peaceful, if I took a bunch of Tylenol? I'm really sensitive to it and one pill usually knocks me out. Would it be like going to sleep?

These thoughts pervaded my mind in rapid succession. What gave me pause, what shifted the experience, was fear...Fear that if I attempted to kill myself and I was unsuccessful that I would be placed into a mental institution and be officially classified as "crazy," as "mentally unstable."

I placed the bottle of Tylenol back onto the bureau and left the room. Not long after that I chose to leave with my children, left, and filed for divorce.

The fear of staying in that relationship had become greater than the fear of leaping into the unknown. The fear of staying had become greater than the fear and the anxiety of wondering *how on earth* I was going to get through this and support my children.

Part of opening ourselves up to receiving abundance comes from a willingness to trust and have faith in the unknown.

Everything seems to have a way of working itself out, and eventually, abundance found its way back into my heart again.

Transitioning into being a single parent/head of household was one of the most intense growth experiences of my life. There were massive ups and downs, challenges and moments of beautiful ease and grace.

The first few months were rough. I was in survival mode. I had times when I wondered if I had it in me to raise these two boys. I wondered if they would be better off with someone more "fit" to be their mother than me. I was in so much emotional pain, so overwhelmed, that I pushed myself to get out of bed each morning. There were days when the emotional pain and anxiety were so intense that I would cry and cry and cry.

After a terrible car accident, the emotional pain also began to manifest as extreme physical pain. I couldn't walk for long periods of time. I couldn't sit for long. I had to hold my head with one hand whenever I washed my hair. But, it wasn't over...following the recommendation of medical authorities, I continued to practice yoga.

Big mistake. What was that about listening to your inner global navigation system? What was that about listening to your intuition and not giving your power away? Hadn't I learned that lesson yet?

It was during a yoga workshop that things shifted drastically for me. You see, I was a yoga addict. And, during the practice of yoga, rather than letting my emotions flow, I stuffed them down inside of myself. I swallowed them whole, like a gaping maw of death. Until, I broke. I broke myself. During one pose, I partially dislocated my left hip. It was a complete and utter "Oh, shit" moment.

I went from being in pain to *really* being in pain. Walking was a challenge. Sitting or driving, forget it. Forward fold? You have got to be kidding me!

It took me three years before most of the pain went away. During that time, I gave my power, and *thousands* of dollars, to professionals who were convinced that they could help me. Hearing that my body was so dysfunctional it was a wonder I was walking and not in a wheelchair. My spirit was broken.

But it didn't break me down; it broke me open. It was then that I chose to take a stand for myself. There was no way I was willing to give up.

We have a choice to view experiences as happening *to us*, or as happening *for us*. What was the gift in my suffering?

About three years into my recovery, I met a practitioner in New Jersey who managed to reduce my pain by 80 percent in just *one* visit. What most struck me during that appointment was his asking what one of my biggest emotional challenges was.

Oh dear. I knew it was what I had experienced during my marriage and my divorce. Pandora's Box had just been opened. All of the emotions I was feeling, all of the feelings of profound self-doubt, lack of worth, lack of self-confidence, toxic shame, blame, and guilt, were rising to the surface for me to see and feel.

Choosing to dive into my own internal *Bog of Eternal Stench* was my big turning point.

Consciously choosing to peel back the layers of my own doom-doing propelled me forward into where I am today. My secret sauce? Choosing to look at my shit, seeing what was there, and facing it head on, even though parts of me felt terrified. Truly learning how to love *all* parts of myself—even the parts I saw as unworthy, undesirable, unlovable, dirty, and starving.

True abundance begins with choosing to fully accept and love oneself.

Yes, we may have a tendency to define abundance based on financial status. However, financial status has been shown to count for *only 10 percent* of our happiness!

What's in the secret sauce? Come close. I'll tell you. "Experts" will try to sell you on the best this and the best that at helping you to make money, to look like the millionaires you see on social media posing on their islands in front of their luxury yachts, with their private jets in the background, on how to make six figures in one month, and so on.

Psst...there is no recipe to the secret sauce. In my opinion, abundance comes from learning to rise head over heels in love with yourself—all of yourself, especially the parts of yourself that you feel most ashamed about.

It comes from believing and radiating from your heart, *I am worthy, I AM good enough, I AM a badass*. Abundance comes from choosing to claim your seat on your throne of sovereignty and adjusting your crown. Abundance requires believing that you have access to unlimited resources and that you are worthy of and *willing* to receive them.

Abundance is built on self-love and a willingness to alchemize all aspects of life that are out of alignment with your highest potential and the greatest expression of your human self.

When I chose to move out of the energy of victim-hood, shame, and blame and instead chose to stand in my sovereignty, reclaim my personal power, and call bullshit on myself and my limiting beliefs, I chose to love myself. The doors opened and I finally knew how to receive.

I turned around to face myself and discovered that life offers endless opportunities for abundance and prosperity. It all began with learning how to love myself as I am, with believing in myself again. My two sons have grown into amazing, loving, and kind-hearted young men who aren't afraid to express themselves or voice their opinions. The clients I work with are inspiring, fun, and adventurous. My relationships continue to grow and change as I surround myself with people who choose to live in a realm of infinite possibility, where we're excited to see each other grow and create a positive ripple effect upon the world. I have the opportunity to give to other people through the service-based retreats I offer. Furthermore, I practice the art of giving through social entrepreneurship, where a minimum of five percent of each one-on-one sacred exchange is donated to a humanitarian or environmental cause.

You, too, are capable of experiencing prosperity and abundance that goes far beyond finances and material possessions. You, too, have the capability to fall madly in love with yourself and experience your personal well-spring of intrinsic happiness. You, too, have the ability to take action every day toward creating a fulfilling and prosperous life of your dreams.

What are you waiting for? The time is now.

Amanda Leigh is a High Performance Mentor and Mindset Coach. As a single mother of two amazing young men *as well as* an entrepreneur, she understands the unique demands and stressors of balancing business and personal life.

She has used a variety of holistic modalities to move through pain, stress, and fear after leaving an emotionally abusive marriage, recover from physical injury after a car accident and debilitating yoga injury, and become a powerful advocate for her children.

She excels at helping high performers reduce stress, increase their intrinsic happiness, and develop more intimate relationships.

Amanda has been studying and practicing the art of personal growth, movement, and relationships for the past twenty-three years. In 2014, she became a Certified Holistic Lifestyle Coach with the CHEK Institute. She is also a Certified Yoga Teacher, movement teacher, and humanitarian. At the heart of her work, Amanda has a desire to connect people to the core of who they are through a multidimensional approach to healing, rooted in traditional wisdom and modern arts.

Amanda has had the opportunity to work directly or indirectly with some incredible mentors, including Debi Adams, Tommy Thompson, JP Sears, Desiree Rumbaugh, Marc St. Pierre, Paul Chek, Benny Fergusson, Jeffrey Slayter, Kane Minkus, and Ronnie Landis. She continues to explore her edge, learning new and cutting-edge methodologies combining ancient wisdom with modern science geared toward helping people live happier, healthier lives full of purpose. Learn more at **amandaleighpatti.com.**

Special Gift

Visit **www.amandaleighpatti.com** to receive Amanda's 3-part video series on gratitude: "Shift your World Through One Powerful Practice".

A Pilgrimage to Prosperity: Discovering True Value and the Power of a Kind Heart

BY MEGAN LUTHER

Living without passion or purpose was slowly sucking the life out of me. I can vividly remember dealing with a client upset about a project status that I had escalated to his leadership team. He hadn't delivered on his terms of our contract and when he discovered that this was being reported, he became verbally abusive and conducted himself in an incredibly immature and offensive manner. His aggravation only grew as I calmly listed the opportunities we had given him to inform his boss himself and the numerous times we had reached out to help support him with this work. He began to blame me and my team, question my authority, and comment on my abilities as a female in a management position. Finally, as I continued to keep my composure and not react or fire back, he called me a *cunt*. This should have shaken me, I should have felt every possible emotion under the sun, but instead, I felt nothing. I was well aware of how offensive and disrespectful this was, but my reaction at that moment, was numb. Ultimately, that is what caught my attention and woke me up. How had my life come to this? How could I be so apathetic and emotionless? Nothing really seemed to matter to me.

Up to that point, climbing the corporate ladder had completely consumed me. My sense of personal power was distorted as a result of working in a male dominated, old-school-boys-club type industry. I had achieved a standard of success for myself—I "worked hard to play hard"...but really, I was just exhausted and miserable. I had no idea how to slow down or be present, I avoided being alone, and I couldn't remember what I was working so hard *for*. Even though I was good at my job and success came easy, I didn't enjoy what I was doing at all.

I knew I needed a change, but my mind could not fully accept it. It wanted to keep pushing through because that's what I had always known. Instead, my body took action and began to shut down. I started having multiple, intense anxiety attacks each week where I would be immobilized and unable to speak. When traveling, I would break out in hives as I arrived at the airport or if I was running late and was scared I'd miss my flight.

I became socially awkward and couldn't find the fun-loving extrovert inside that everyone had always described me to be. I remember plastering my back against a wall at a holiday party, hoping no one would see me and being absolutely terrified to speak to people I knew very well. In that moment it became painfully clear how truly unhappy I had become in all aspects of my life. I had isolated myself and was full of self doubt and regret for not doing the things I really wanted to do. I was not living the life I wanted to live. I was full of sorrow after so much time spent looking outside of myself for answers. I questioned every decision I had made, how I had chosen to fill my time, and my incessant need to stay busy.

It seemed ironic to be so unhappy and yet surrounded by so much prosperity in the form of financial abundance and corporate success.

"Try not to become a person of success, but
rather try to become a person of value."

—ALBERT EINSTEIN

I was independent, well respected, and valued at my firm. Nevertheless, promotions felt meaningless and I worked long hours each week, which included most weekends. I was always focused on the next project and the next performance cycle, never coming up for air or celebrating the moment I was in. Completely exhausted, depressed, and lost, I was searching externally for validation of who I was and what I was doing. I wanted someone else to give me these answers, and my focus was very much on "doing" and not "being." I was lonely, with a feeling of emptiness I hadn't been aware of before. I had worked hard to reach this level of success for myself, but in the process, I forfeited all connection to my inner landscape.

Late one night, after my most severe anxiety attack, I had an incredible and excruciating experience. I was completely awake and embodied, but watching what I would describe as a mental movie. I relived hundreds of thoughts, words and actions that had occurred throughout my life in which I was not being my best self. These were situations I had forgotten about, brushed aside or buried deep within, but every sorry example came to the surface for me to feel again from a completely different perspective. It was as if my senses were heightened—I could see and feel the effect my actions had on others. It made my stomach hurt to see and feel it all back to back with such shame and remorse. Slowly, I began to see themes—the cycles of hurting others when I felt vulnerable and the lengths I went to avoid being hurt myself.

I was watching this personal portrayal—me at my absolute worst—for what felt like an eternity. I saw every selfish choice, every immoral decision, and each and every time I had hurt another to put myself first. This night completely changed my life. I wept like never before. It was extremely difficult to endure but now I can see how it helped reveal the illusions and the falsities of the life I had created. I saw exactly what I was being and it could not have been more clear to me, I knew I did not want to be that person anymore. I realized that I was only able to recognize my value through the lens of what I *did*—my occupation and the "productive" aspect of my life. I needed the credentials behind my name and my boss-lady title to define me—because at my foundation, my presence was not enough. I needed other people to validate my worth.

So I dug deeper into the internal programming and limiting beliefs that I carried. In my mind, it was impossible to be prosperous and abundant without giving up my soul's calling and working 100+ hours a week. The foundation of this belief system was built from a childhood premise that I was unwanted, not good enough and that I would always be rejected. My biological father had left our small town when he found out my mother was pregnant and I had spent most of my life preparing for his return. I worked hard to make something of myself so that when he did come back, I could show him everything that he missed out on and prove that, despite his absence, I had worth. He never did come back. I see now how those toxic beliefs contributed to my strive for perfection, my need for external validation, and the constant feeling that I was never doing enough. Nothing ever truly felt satisfying, because I was doing it for someone else.

I had bought into this illusion for years and continually compared myself to other people's success, and their measures of power and contribution. I found it so easy to diminish myself and my role and to resort to the endless fear of failure. In my mind, I would never measure up. This way of thinking supported my role as a high-performing consultant—always working really hard and doing more than what was required, but it kept my true gifts hidden and my passion and creativity stifled. I was disconnected, unhealthy and very unhappy.

> "The deepest secret is that life is not a process of discovery, but a process of creation. You are not discovering yourself, but creating yourself anew. Seek therefore, not to find out Who You Are, but seek to determine Who You Want To Be."
>
> —*NEALE DONALD WALSCH*

At times, I still struggle to transcend the constant pressure and expectation to "do" rather than just allowing myself to "be". It took effort to change my frame of reference and value my worth, but finally, I have accepted that my value does not come from what I do on the outside. It doesn't matter how the world reacts or views me as long as I am being true to myself.

After my experience of awakening, I began exploring the undeniable spiritual energy that was rising up in me. I had a heightened sense of awareness and deeper sense of knowing. I became aware of synchronicities everywhere. In meditation I would pose questions that would somehow be answered soon after, and I felt strongly connected, supported and guided through my transformation. I re-prioritized and contemplated the meaning of life and the value of a peaceful existence, becoming confident in the simplicity of it all.

I felt an overwhelming sense of trust which allowed me to look within and open myself up to experience more. I slowly dissolved the walls I had built to surround my heart, which had helped me avoid pain but also kept me from fully feeling joy and receiving love. I redefined my capacity to experience and express love. I *remembered* my true essence and embraced the presence of love that I now offer, and that is enough for me. I don't need to be or do anything else. This is when I truly know I am in my power—when I choose to fully accept my presence and own my own vibration. It comes from who I am *being*, rather than what I do.

Becoming truly abundant has meant letting go of what was safe and secure and exploring my infinite Self. It has been a process of learning to see past the illusions of our society and choosing to redefine this structure for myself—to see myself as whole and believing in a deep inner knowing that the possibilities are endless if I continue to follow my heart.

Prosperity has shifted from a focus of success related to financial stability to a flourishing and thriving condition of self and personal well-being.

I've decluttered and downsized, surrounding myself with only the items that make me truly happy, that I appreciate and love having. I focus now on the experience of my day and of my life, instead of just trying to push through it. Surrendering to the wholeness that I am.

From that earlier place of emptiness, I learned exactly what I am not and I let it all go: the titles, the people and things in my life that did not nourish my soul. I let go of the expectations I had for myself and for what my life *should* look like. Even more difficult, was letting go of the expectations others had for me and the reactions and criticism that soon followed.

The hardest lesson was overcoming the guilt and the shame I felt for making such a selfish decision, a decision that I knew would have a drastic impact on my fiancée. Leaving my job and the substantial income it provided affected his quality of life and his lifestyle. I likely would have made the decision to quit a lot sooner than I did, had I not had another person to consider. I felt awful that I was so unhappy and I felt selfish for making a choice that would change his life too. We had a vision for our life together and I was the one who wanted to change—this meant a lot of our shared goals would have to be postponed. It also put a significant amount of additional stress on him as his income alone would need to afford our life and he would need to provide for us while I figured myself out.

So, it wasn't just me who had to defend my choice to others and answer the uncomfortable questions, he had to as well. It hurt my heart to know that the ones that loved and supported him most began to worry about him and question whether I was still the right person for him. Ultimately, the decision to leave my job brought up a lot of fear and a lot of commentary; the most common being "I could/would never do that", "how could you leave your job without having something else lined up", "you must be crazy", "you've lost your mind" and "you're having a midlife crisis". It was hard enough for me to articulate what I was doing to my now husband, let alone other people. For a long time, I couldn't actually explain everything I was feeling and what I was doing, or what I was going to do and how I was going to make a living, I just knew I was unhappy and couldn't continue to live that way.

What surprised me and still continues to surprise me, is how open my husband is with others about what I am doing. For a long time I was awkward and shy sharing about my interests and spirituality. I would overhear him proudly telling others about me, even though he didn't understand (or believe in!) any of it. At the same time that I was letting go of what was no longer in alignment with who I wanted to be, people were also letting go of me. He stood by me when others could no longer accept me, he supported and encouraged me and sacrificed a lot for me to continue on this path. His confidence and love helped me to move forward and I will be forever grateful to him for our new life together.

I eventually stopped explaining myself to others and made it my mission to find a happiness that was not conditional to my external world. I stepped onto my path as a seeker—seeking a new way of looking at the world, hoping to find greater understanding of who I really was and the passion that would fuel my life's work.

I focused on what resonated with my heart, paying attention to the feelings I would receive in my body and what brought me joy and lit me up inside. It was a process of relearning what felt right, even if it didn't make logical sense. When I felt this resonance—the deep inner experience of knowing—I trusted it. I listened. I paid attention to what I was attracted to and the synchronicities that would show up. From this space, I unlocked my inherent spirituality, reconnecting with myself and trusting that I was supported. I opened to higher Self and higher purpose, tuning inward to discover what I needed to create my dreams as a reality.

Now truth, when I know it or hear it, vibrates through my body and sends shivers up my spine, resonating on the deepest level of my being.

My feeling navigation and intuition have been my most important guides to trust and follow. If ever uncertain, I pause and sit in silence, waiting for deeper truth to emerge. It always shows up, and the more I tap in, the easier it comes. I feel into what is real for me in each moment and the first instinct that comes. My deepest feelings have brought me to my highest truth, cultivating a relationship with the purity and passion in my heart.

I honor my heart by following its guidance, trusting its truth, even when it feels risky.

This journey has helped me to realize the value of true emptiness. What was once an empty, lonely feeling in my being has been alchemized into a practice of *empty presence*—letting go of all that does not serve me, knowing what is real for me in each moment, and feeling into the wholeness of my being.

The magic is inside me; the magic I am seeking is who I am.

Before this transformation (which I have now accepted as never-ending!), I struggled to own my gifts and truly value my self-worth. Now, it is a daily practice to consciously choose to focus on a positive sense of self and to let go of judgment, and it seems to get easier every day. Nurturing myself and cultivating love and worthiness in my heart elevates my vibration and allows me to truly honor my gifts. It supports me in appreciating these qualities enough to share them with others.

I continue to deepen into love and allow myself to be truly seen, especially as I start my own energy healing practice. At first, I worried people in my old life would judge me, thinking I had lost my mind and fell off in the spiritual deep end. Well, the truth is...I *did* lose my mind by letting go of my critical ego mind and fully embracing the ONE voice of my highest Self.

I also experienced fear that people in my holistic healing community would not accept me, believing I was not capable or equipped to share healing work because I was a corporate convert. This thinking sent me straight into self-doubt where every insecurity would surface. I felt into the unworthiness and fear of rejection, the mistrust of myself and the fear of uncertainty. I realized this mindset kept me silent, kept me small, and, for a long time, kept me from contributing.

My truth is simply recognizing that I am a kind person and have a kind heart. I have the confidence to own the vibration of love in my heart and acknowledge the power that one kind heart has on this planet. I've learned to value this presence and come from this expansive place into service. Holding the space for more love for myself allows me to hold deeper presence for others to heal. It often means holding space for silence. The transmission of love is in our presence, and I humbly accept the simplicity and sacredness of love as the truth of my being.

I believe we're here to learn to own our unique gifts, to share these qualities with others and to hold this part of ourselves as sacred. If we can see our true essence and come from this place in our offerings, we can only thrive and be supported by the Universe. When we have integrity and offer only what resonates for us, we can trust ourselves to be in a space of authentic heart service to others. When we create our days, living sacred, giving praise for the richness and blessings we have, sharing flows naturally and we can accept the mystery as a part of the harmony of our lives.

This is true authentic power and prosperity. This kind of power radiates in every single one of us; we just need to value it for ourselves and allow it to move through us. If we can act in accordance with divine wisdom with intention toward our highest good, we can learn to live and love in balance. Society has long used power for control and domination, yet if we learn a new system of interaction for ourselves, we can make an impact on the world. If we are individually willing to change, the collective will shift. We accept responsibility for our actions and our thoughts and use our power wisely—as power *to,* not power *over.* If we each nurture peace and enlightenment within ourselves, and we don't act from greed and anger, the most powerful acts are then acts of love that come directly from our hearts.

Being able to see myself and make offerings from this authentic space of power creates flow, and creates opportunities for connection in my outer world. I honor this empowerment in me as my new foundation. Now, I move forward with the pure intention to connect with others from the heart and share vulnerably without expectation of anything in return.

> "Someone I loved once gave me a box full
> of darkness. It took me years to understand
> that this too, was a gift."
>
> *-MARY OLIVER*

As I build my capacity to see beyond life's illusions, each trigger I experience becomes a new opportunity, an initiation to come into more love, to shed what does not serve me and continue to choose the path of prosperity.

My practice is to stay present with my core beliefs, transmute old subconscious patterning by staying present and aware of my thoughts, and to move through fear by choosing love when I am challenged. This means choosing to stay in my light and to always come from a place of compassion, honoring myself and being honest when I am out of alignment. I gracefully call myself back into my truth, without judgment and with sincere kindness. I take ownership for my human mishaps and I give myself permission to do better in the future. The admission of what feels wrong calls me back into my personal power. The acknowledgment alone begins to shift the negative energy. This simple self-confession and reflection of how I've shown up recognizes the misalignment of my actions to who I know I am and who I want to be for the world. Sovereignty is available with each mistake, as another opportunity to integrate more parts of myself back into wholeness.

Being on the path of true prosperity requires continually calling in more truth of who I really am, and finding compassion and love for myself in the moments when I sway off—and then recognizing that I have the power to choose differently. It's a commitment to my higher self that I deeply honor. Life's initiations are an offering; let us see them for the gifts they are and embrace what we can learn by truly receiving them.

This period of self-transformation has been an intense process of letting go and getting real with what is in my heart. I needed to release all outcomes and expectations, to see and be grateful for the beauty and abundance surrounding me now. I used to look for distractions from my pain, and now I have cultivated the courage to lean into it, learning to alchemize the fear, the pain, and the separation to let myself be truly seen. Feeling full of life, full of love, and full of Self, in a non-egoic or arrogant way, has been the truest form of prosperity for me.

> "Love is the ultimate state of human
> behavior where compassion prevails
> and kindness rules."
>
> —YOGI BHAJAN

I now embrace all that I am; I see all qualities, the light and the shadow, and I know that all are necessary and loved. I know what I truly desire, and who I am for others—and my own presence empowers me.

A thriving sense of self and the spaciousness in my heart have brought new experiences, new people, and new depths of feeling into my life. Each connection is richer and more meaningful because I am awakened to my true Self, and my heart is open to receive myself, to receive others and the full experience of life. This richness stems from coming out of hiding, sharing my truth without fear of judgment and without comparison.

I practice daily gratitude and praise for all that I do receive, knowing that abundance is present when I honor myself and lovingly receive every part of this life that surrounds me. Time is now my most appreciated asset. I deeply value the freedom I feel each day, the simple things that feed my soul. The happiness. The peace of mind. The beauty of the surrender. The mystery of it all.

Once we recognize that the highest vibration of prosperity is love, we receive *everything*. Prosperity is in us, a part of us, and we can access it anytime—as love.

Love is the most powerful human experience and we are each able to define what love is for ourselves and how we want to show up in this life. As a collective, isn't it time to feel just how expansive and powerful our love truly runs?! The river of love and prosperity I carry for myself—for us all—runs deep and unconditional.

Megan Luther lives in Bragg Creek, Canada with her husband Daniel. She is a mind-body intuitive and a meditation guide, working with clients using several energy healing modalities. She is certified in ThetaHealing™, Reiki and reading Akashic Records and uses alchemical crystal singing bowls in both her one-on-one sessions as well as her group classes and workshops. Megan is passionate about sharing in the awareness and expansion of our consciousness. She is inspired to experience meaningful life in community and to support others in dissolving limiting beliefs, transforming the ego personality, and coming into a deeper remembrance of their true essence. Learn more at **www.highhearthealing.love.**

Special Gift

Yoga Nidra is a systematic relaxation practice and guided meditation to expanded states of the field of consciousness, beyond the five senses. This wisdom teaching is a portal into one's authentic nature, where the timeless self resides. Megan offers a 50-minute experience for your exploration at **www.highhearthealing.love/prosperity.**

Trust is My Savings Account

BY MIA LUZ

She is calling.

She is summoning Her children back home.
Are you hearing Her call?
Are you heeding Her call?

Mama Gaia's call is being heard by many and more.
I smile.
All is well.

As a culture we have lost our connection to nature—our provider, our teacher, and our security. The seduction of the prescribed path is powerful, leading us away from our hearts, making it possible for us to disconnect with our Mother, She who is our abundance and our Earth. I had to detour and get lost in the realms of our cultural disconnect and fear paradigm before I could understand this.

I remember saying as a teenager that I didn't want to be rich, I wanted to live a rich life! Little did I know, what you ask for you shall receive. A rich life it became, for sure, navigating adventures, creativity, the endless search for meaning and truth, abuse, love, despair, loss, abundance, and bliss...and I have not become rich, yet. I knew somewhere deep within that money alone would not make me happy or fulfilled.

So I set out to not make my fortune.

RECURRING DREAM

When my daughter was three I started having a recurring lucid dream of my Maya (a.k.a. my live-in Guru) and me holding hands, skipping joyfully toward the horizon through a barren desert. Going nowhere. Coming from nowhere. Empty handed. Completely content, happy and fulfilled, radiating grace, joy, and love. This dream was a saving grace for what was to come.

My wake-up call was a stripping of everything that I thought I was and had. Knowing the stories are unimportant, though they do serve a purpose when seeing the opportunities within them. These alchemizing situations initiate us into higher frequencies.

One of my greatest gifts and initiations came through an undiagnosed chronic illness: two years in bed as a single mother with minimal help. Many sleepless nights of worry and anxiety trying to figure out a solution in my external reality.

With a humble child support check I somehow made it work, riding the wings of my creativity. I would tell myself that I was mastering the ability to dilute money. No one really knew how little we had, as I never projected lack or poverty, keeping my head up high at the assistance office. Always knowing the worth of my soul, I chose to walk with dignity and integrity through my days, even when faced with custody battles, illness, bankruptcy, heartbreak, and not knowing if I could make it through. Having experienced domestic violence, I understood that I am never a victim and can always take radical responsibility for my situation—and I knew deep in my heart I had created my situation for a reason. I was in the maze of the Dark Goddess. Only I did not, at the time, fully understand why.

Why was I swirling in this maze? Because it was time. My cleaning the slate time. My stripping of everything time. Total surrendering time. Eradicating viral social conditioning time. It was awakening time.

I was slowly freeing myself from the fear of being without. Slowly able to let go of the illusion of having security. Having nothing is freedom, because there is nothing to lose. Then you can build from there...it's a win-win. I was gifted a clear slate.

All was still. All was empty.

There was nothing to do. There was nowhere to go...

...but *within*...to be present with each moment.

Ahhhh the refuge. This was the why.

My soul was aroused. I was finally still enough to hear Her. Quiet enough to feel Her. Present enough to *be* with Her. From my bed I could hear *Her* breathing. Waking up to trust.

The "*dream*" became my safe haven, my emotional security. I knew we were always going to be okay.

I listened...

...then there was a call. It was Gaia, our Earth Star herself. She had come to lead me into the experience of true freedom.

I was ready.

She offered me a gift in the form of a multi-purpose channel. I was to become a drum doula and make medicine drums.

What? Me? Make drums?

Yes, me. I was to create Her heartbeat so that many and more can hear Her call. I was to assist others in the birthing of their own drums, their own heartbeats. Sounding Mama Gaia's heartbeat into our mass confusion. She gifted the transmission to me so that I could find my way to my purpose.

The drums became the vehicle on my road to healing
and inner abundance—abundance that I cannot lose.
Soul-level healing.

Spirit is always presenting us with opportunities that are in alignment with our purpose and highest potential; all I had to do was learn how to listen, trust, and follow. This time I did. I had no more fear. Nothing holding me back. Slowly it all started to unfold. Still and ever unfolding.

This gift was a merging of all that I am. Since childhood I have worked with my hands in every possible medium. I have always been a seeker of spirit and I am a Leo and a number one in numerology, making me a natural leader. This channel uses all of me, all that I love and all that I am naturally good at. I can offer the fullness of who I am.

As the unfolding took place, I eventually figured out that it was chronic Lyme I was battling. I found a healer who was able to guide me back to complete health after seven years of illness. People, situations, opportunities, and

Gaia came forth on my path, teaching me that when the body fails it enables the soul to thrive, get stronger and lead the way. This is powerful medicine. Now I know I am to be a bridge between nature and culture.

Somewhere in the midst of it all I made it through to the "other side," free of the shackles our culture forces upon us, free of the programming of what success means, free of fear, lack, worry...Finding myself fulfilled, abundant, peaceful and with joy. This truly feels like happiness—non-circumstantial happiness. The gratitude, the beauty, the awe of creation that is my reality. An underlying bliss between the moments that make up my life. Fully trusting in the guidance of my higher self, knowing this part of me has full connection with all of creation, both in the seen and unseen worlds. My connection to spirit is strong.

I am still a single mother, still financially living under normal standards in America, driving the same car, living in the same home...But, I am abundant beyond words. *Truly abundant.* My home is beautiful, a temple in its purest form, my sanctuary. I have a thriving garden that has shown me more generosity than I thought possible. We graciously make it through the winters by stoking the wood-stove, feeding our souls at the same time. We have a beautiful like-minded community filled with endless support and unconditional love. This is proving to me that our whole life is determined by our inner state. The health of our Soul. As within so without.

Today I have banished my teenage words, "I don't want to be rich, I want to live a rich life" and instead *welcome* financial abundance and prosperity through sacred economy where purpose and abundance meet. Maybe I'll even have a savings account made up of numbers one day! Though I will not compromise myself or betray my soul for riches, as soul health is my highest priority. My channel widens. Paying it forward. Giving back of the abundance I've learned of. Knowing that the drum birthing is all but a stepping stone in the unfolding. Inspired to continue my search for purpose and offering...and yet this abundance is only part of me.

There are other parts wanting to be healed, integrated and balanced into this reality. There's the part of me that has not yet figured out how to create *financial* abundance. The part that is difficult to even express since it is still a mystery to me. I don't think money would increase my well-being or joy, or my capacity to love, or the magnitude of my light. Yet I am ready to reconcile. There is so much more within Her teachings of abundance. When we honor Her she can in turn provide the wealth she is so willing to share. The wealth that fulfills and nourishes us on every level. She has no judgment, no discrimination and is always unconditionally loving.

There is always enough.

Being in right relationship with Her, ourselves, our purpose, our surroundings, abundance and yes, money, She opens up Her floodgates. I believe when we can create our lives from this place, what money we receive and spend carries a different vibration, bringing a higher consciousness and striving for the highest good. We step out from the ordinary way. We choose nature. We choose love. We choose humanity. We choose our future. We step into our power, where expectations of our culture and others no longer dictate our lives. We create freedom. And in freedom is abundance.

Mia Luz is an ever-unfolding mystic, truth-seeker, and spiritual electrician. She's a devotee of Earth mother and midwife of Spirit, empowering seekers to find their way back to their essence, true purpose, and soul fulfillment. Mia blesses through the medicine of the West, the women's lodge, where the deep, dark, primal and watery territory of feminine flow lies. Her deep connection to Earth was sparked growing up on a farm in Sweden, and her ongoing travels and studies in cultures with earth-based religions, ancient traditions, and plant medicines have stoked her profound wisdom. She serves as a ceremonial guide who can create an atmosphere outside of time and space. Being a seasoned facilitator, Mia deeply understands the magic of coming together supporting one another to heal and awaken. She focuses on supporting the New Earth frequencies by assisting hundreds in the process of finding their way back to nature, their voice, and their spirit through the birthing of their own drums in ceremony. Mia enables her students to release the shackles of old belief systems and cultural programming to ultimately thrive in their own light. Her clients evolve into a space of deeper trust, self-love, and true inner emotional freedom. Mia offers a compassionate, safe and nonjudgmental space for deep transformation and liberation through workshops, ceremonies, circles, retreats, and online channels through which she uses community-based coaching to inspire the collective. Learn more at **drumdoula.com.**

Losing It All to Find My True Self

BY MARIBETH MORRISSEY

As a young girl I can remember one of my favorite things to do was go in my neighbors' driveway and pick out the most oddly and uniquely shaped stones and shine them in my friend's stone machine. It made them so beautiful and smooth—I witnessed the transformation from strange and ugly to smooth and beautiful.

This transformation seems to reflect the essence of my life—experiencing the messiness of pain and suffering, but then choosing to surrender into the moment and finding beauty inside of the suffering.

This beautiful suffering has transformed grief into forgiveness and has facilitated my rebirth. I have chosen to learn and grow from each experience and allow death to usher in rebirth. I have released the need to fix others and am so much closer to aligning with and remembering my true self. Now, I am asking myself the big questions: *Who am I? And why did I choose to be here?*

This path of beautiful suffering that found me has become my calling. *It has become my path to abundance.*

As far back as I can remember, my uncle and parents' friends were saying, "She's got it." I was happy and loved to make others smile. I didn't understand until later that it meant aligning with my purpose and light. Then, I had dreams and ideals of a perfect life. I played the dating game and believed the perfect man would come and provide the perfect life for me. I loved

Cinderella, but, more importantly, I vowed as a young girl to never have a marriage like my parents.

I remember the endless days and nights of putting the pillow over my head to drown out the sounds. My dad would play in the band at night, then go to his girlfriend's house. I remember my mom following him—and the fighting afterward. Oh, I *vowed* to find my prince, the one who would save me.

I didn't realize the mirror that my life growing up would provide for me as I got older, but it certainly has. Early on, I didn't have tools or parents to teach me how to live differently, so I had many painful lessons to learn.

The youngest of five, I had a sister who was mentally challenged—and was my best friend. I learned so much about unconditional love from her. She was teased relentlessly, and I felt her anguish. She repeatedly tried to commit suicide and I would try to make her happy and get her to stop. When the ambulance would come I would sit behind the curtain and pray that they could pump her stomach and get the sleeping pills out. I went to visit her in the psychiatric ward. "I will find a way to get you out," I whispered in her ear.

Sometimes, I would get away to a relatives house and dance in their basement. It was here that a family member sexually abused me. I thought it must be my fault that he was interested in me. He told me not to tell anyone or I could never come back. My teenage years were out of control, dominated by sex, drugs, and a physically abusive relationship. From the ages of fourteen through seventeen, my life was filled with terror. I lost friends because they were afraid they would get hurt. He even pulled a gun out and said if I left him he would kill himself. After much counseling and with the support of a male friend who protected me, I finally broke free.

I grew up being mad at my dad and feeling my mom's pain—and the responsibility to make her happy. I was told I was the best accident to be born. My brother, who was five years older than me, had a friend named Patrick who came around, and my mom would say, to me, "He's the one for you." He was my brother's best friend and over the years he became mine, too. I thought of him as a brother, but one with whom I could share my deepest feelings—he was a good listener. I dated a lot, mostly older men who made me feel safe, but Patrick was always there as my rock. It wasn't until my senior year in college that Patrick stopped calling—I didn't know why. I asked him why and what was going on, and he said, "I love the hell out of you." I asked why it had taken him so long to tell me, and he said he'd been waiting for me to feel the same.

I knew he was the man for me. He produced horse shows around the country, and he literally swept me off my feet, like a prince from a fairytale. Our life of living large had began.

I moved to Florida, got married, and started my new life. We lived on an island with professional baseball and hockey players and prominent doctors as our neighbors. We drove fancy cars, took our kids to every activity from swimming to baseball, and even had a nanny. I worked as a pharmaceutical rep, but after having our first two children of four, decided to stay home. We had a vacation home and rental properties and spent our summers up north where we'd grown up. We called the vacation home "the little house," and we all loved it. Still, the things we accumulated never seemed like enough. I yearned to be closer to my family and our "little house."

We decided to move back home and built an even bigger home than the one we had. While we were completing this 10,000-square-foot home, Patrick had a mini stroke. This was the first in a series of changes that rocked my world. I began to suffer with depression and allergies. A doctor asked me how I handled stress. *What stress?,* I thought, *I live in a multi-million dollar home and drive a fancy car.*

I started seeing a therapist. Everything that I had ever suppressed from the past surfaced—and boy did I *dislike* myself. In the first session, my therapist asked me to look in the mirror and say, I love you, but I couldn't do it. I cried. After several sessions of healing, I knew there was more than just physical reasons for my illness, and I had an intense desire to learn more. I flew to Chicago to meet Dr. Darren Weissman and started taking classes. Over the course of several years of learning with Dr. Weissman, I became a Certified Lifeline Practitioner. I knew that I had to do this to not only help me and my family but others who were suffering. It was a way to access buried emotions and beliefs, process them and align with your true self. It was here that the traumas came up to be healed from the sexual and physical abuse from age eight through my teens.

Enormous shifts were happening within me. We moved six times, downsizing each time, selling real estate and stocks and turning in pensions. And then my mother was diagnosed with pancreatic cancer. My beliefs about medicine had been evolving, while other family members trusted only Western medicine. And, just as I was losing my mother, I found distance growing between myself and my siblings. My intuition grew stronger, as I heard and saw signs from my mom and what I recognized as God. Even so, losing her was profoundly painful.

A few years later, my dad was also diagnosed with pancreatic cancer. *No chemo,* he told me. *Only piano and family.* That's what would make him want to live. My siblings had a lot of anger and resentment about his decision, and I hadn't even spoken to two of my siblings since our mother's death and our disagreement about how to treat a loved one with cancer. During this time I learned about forgiveness and about hospice.

Hospice was brought in, and, honestly, it was an immense relief to have more emotional support and nurses who could come in and care for him. I could focus on being his daughter. It was really in these last months and weeks that I was able to forgive my dad and to forgive myself for closing myself off from loving him for all these years. He told me what it was like for him and expressed himself for the first time. I got to know my dad in a whole new way. I loved him—not how he'd treated my mom, but I understood more and was able to hold compassion for him. This was the key to forgiveness, and I realized then (like a blueprint) that it all starts with self-compassion, and then can spread outward into the family, the community, and the larger world.

Just before my dad transitioned, he promised that if I went into hospice work he would help me with other families from his new vantage point. I never imagined this would be the road I was on. But what a gift it has been! To be able to see life and death, and help other families and patients surrender into the unknown with faith, acceptance, and forgiveness. It is such a powerful mirror for my life.

After my dad's passing, I noticed tension in my marriage. Patrick lost his job and struggled to find another that would stick. He didn't like what he was doing and felt his choices were limited. In addition to seeing coaching clients, I had a part-time job at a health food store. But, now, suddenly I needed to go back to work full time. After interviewing for several months with pharmaceutical jobs that never worked out, I got a call from a neighbor who referred me to a hospice company that hired me as a patient care coordinator.

The magic of hospice is the mirror into transition and death, and offers the realization that parts of us are dying every day. Do we resist or surrender into change? This was *just* the inquiry I needed.

For so long I was angry because my life was *not* reflecting the fairy tale life I signed up for! Patrick was supposed to be the strong money-making man; I was supposed to take care of the home and the kids and have a part time job. Most of my friends and neighbors were pretty well off, and when I compared myself I would get even angrier.

I went to Florida for some support in sacred sisterhood. After meeting up with these amazing women, I realized how different my life had become and how my relationship with my husband had changed. I felt separate and alone and allowed the tears to flow.

I knew I needed to let go of trying to control it all. Control equaled fear. And while I cried and the fear dissolved, I started to see my life come before me like a life review, as if a death were occurring inside of me that I could not stop.

My three friends held my hand and loved me through it. I realized there was no answer, no fixing. It just *was*. After what seemed like a lifetime I picked up my face and said, "There is no more of that old life and belief system. It's gone. I realize my belief that a man should take care of me is not valid anymore. I need to let go and step into a new way of living!"

It was as if a veil of truth had been lifted for me and new door was opening. I was in a safe space of sacredness to allow this new birth of *me* to arrive. Although my intention for the weekend was to feel joy, I just cracked open and the rush of emotion felt raw and challenging—but also empowering and free.

Looking back on it, I realize my prince fell off his horse, and so did I! Patrick was not in my life to *save* me. I've had to learn to trust that *I* am the creator of my life—even though I don't always have the answers. I can *always* trust my faith.

How have I managed to come to this place? As I shift my beliefs, so does my life. It's much easier to turn to food or drink or other substances than to go inward and shift and then let go, trust, and love yourself no matter what is happening in your life. I've learned that the best way is through the pain, trusting and aligning as you go.

Looking back, I am also reminded of my dad's dying process, and of the many hospice patients who I visit, and families who are letting go of their loved ones. Nobody chooses death, but the more we resist, the harder it is. When we let go and surrender, we allow life, and God, to flow through us.

I believe we came to earth knowing our purpose and why we chose to be here. Like praying hands, we are aligned with God and with love. As we experience life's challenges, our truth can slip away. And then we forget why we are here and buy into others beliefs that we are not good enough, pretty enough, smart enough, or rich enough—and maybe even receive an unwanted diagnosis. But the process of letting go and surrendering can be the tipping point for change and the birth of something new.

For the past twelve years, I've been on this awakening journey of losing it all to find my true self—and there is no finish line!

When a friend referred me to Flower of Life Press to write a chapter for this book on prosperity and abundance, I laughed and said, "I'm just the opposite of abundant! I get money and then I lose it over and over!" She encouraged me with the thought that writing may be a way to transform my story of lack and scarcity. I also liked the idea that a percentage of sales would go to the nonprofit Pachamama Alliance to protect indigenous lands and share educational programs with people ready to take bold action.

Every Sunday I tape and watch "Super Soul Sunday" with Oprah and an author. (I always imagine myself sitting in that chair one day!) But on one particular day, my girlfriend texted me urging me to watch it. As I watched it, I thought, this woman and her book *The Soul Of Money* seemed so familiar! It was all about finding true abundance and prosperity— exactly what I've been writing about! I listened to Lynn Twist's story of how much money they had and how it was never enough—I thought she was talking about *my* story!

Lynn Twist also spoke about how she realized true happiness was shar- ing and giving back. She had co-founded the Pachamama Alliance to help feed the hungry. In that moment, I stood frozen with tears and chills. This was a God incidence, a synchronicity, a sign that I was on the right path! This was the charity where a portion of proceeds from our book was going!

With this sign from the universe, I found my flow. I became fully aligned with my purpose. My hands were back together in prayer, remembering my truth. By allowing, forgiving, accepting, letting go, and opening up, this mir- acle had occurred.

I also discovered that when I said yes to contributing to this book that you are now reading, new clients showed up—more families for me to teach about the medicare hospice benefit. What a gift to help families during their most sacred time and to allow God to work through me as fear is removed replaced with love. I've learned so much! My relationship with Patrick has taught me unconditional love, and my persistent anger has been transmuted and dissolved. Life has shown me that a life based on only material possessions is not sustainable and will not bring me the true love, joy, and happiness I am here to experience.

Through this process of losing it all to find my true self, I've also discovered what abundance and prosperity *really* are—and they're not just about dollar bills. So now, I live by these tenets:

Live life to its fullest, as if today was your last day.
Say what you want to say, do the things you want to do.
Forgive more easily.
Tell people you love them.
And give back!

Now, I find the abundance and prosperity within so that I can share it with others—because I know that I cannot give what I don't have! And as I do this practice, the people and situations that I need or desire appear. It's a flow of living your passion and giving back! The shift in perception occurs and I realize, *What if this all were happening* for *me, instead of* to *me?*

Living this practice of compassion, love, and gratitude for self and others allows me to live from my heart. It doesn't feel like "work"—rather, it's an easy way to manifest my desires and it inspires me to help others in need. *This* is true abundance.

Maribeth Morrissey, Author and Life Coach, assists clients in Healing Through Communication with a variety of modalities. She trained directly with Dr. Darren Weissman, developer of The Lifeline Technique, and studied extensively at Hay House events with her mentors Wayne Dyer and Louise Hay. Maribeth has over fifteen years experience in the pharmaceutical industry with training and exposure to traditional medicine. She also serves as an Intuitive, Educator, and Inspirational Speaker on health and end of life topics in the community, and has been a regular contributor to *Woman's Journal* Magazine for over fifteen years while maintaining a growing practice. Maribeth extends a healing presence to help process difficult emotions with love and compassion. During her own challenging experiences, her heart opened and she became a conduit to receive messages from deceased loved ones. She now shares these gifts with her clients as they heal from the inside out. Maribeth also works as a Hospice Patient Care Coordinator, educating families, patients, and the medical community on the Hospice Medicare Benefit. Since losing her own parents, Maribeth has become a passionate advocate to help other families and loved ones receive this life transforming benefit. Learn more at **maribethmorrissey.com**.

Special Gift

Access your FREE video "How To Manifest When You Are Going Through Life Changes and Stress" at **maribethmorrissey.com/free-gift**.

Intuition and Full Spectrum Intelligence: Your Most Powerful Business Assets

BY KATE MULDER

We can't talk about abundance—or, let's be real: money—without recognizing that the world is changing. We are in the middle of a great rewrite, a new framework or a new paradigm. I don't have a magic formula for abundance, and even if there was a formula, it, too, would be changing. As we watch our world economy, our employment structure, our lifestyle, and our human evolution rapidly shift, I want to tell you that you already have tools to help you thrive—tools that you might not even realize you have. I'm going to tell you the story of how my intuition and my access to my full spectrum intelligence—to my great surprise—told me, a California tech worker, to go bolster the economy of Peru. And I did!

My own journey with money has been a rocky one. I grew up in a house where we were taught to be "of service" and there was an underlying belief that rich people don't do good for the world. I received a full tuition scholarship to my dream college, worked hard, and got my dream job at the age of twenty, studying the intelligence of bottlenose dolphins. Out of college, I landed a six-figure sales job. When I had the cash flow, I was good at saving. I didn't think about bills or money and I traveled to where I wanted, visiting more than thirty countries by my late twenties. Turning thirty, I chose a different path. I left my cushy job because I felt I wasn't living my purpose, and I started working for nonprofits and for tech startups who "did good." I've always been passionate about economic development and helping those in developing countries live a better, more empowered life. But I moved so far to the "be of service" spectrum that it became "martyrdom"—not watching out for my own financial needs and ultimately draining my resources. I'm still learning that lesson today. Meanwhile, my higher consciousness told me to travel to a foreign country to bolster its economy. And my intuition aligned me with the right investors, people, teams, and resources when I needed them. It's all been a part of my soul journey—as that's really all everything and anything is...what our soul chooses as part of its evolution.

I have been resisting writing this chapter because I'm again a lower point of my "bank account" due to launching a new business. It's been a doozy of a few months, the biggest energetic and emotional challenge of holding a peaceful and trusting space as my partner and I launch a new paradigm business, one that we know has nine-figure potential—as he holds the keys and wisdom, and solutions for a future that humanity truly needs to thrive as we enter a new paradigm. This solution and wisdom is so powerful and sacred that our incubation and fundraising efforts have been a mix of our own soul journey, our spiritual development, interrelated aspects of divine timing, and the timing of the aligned soul contracts who are meant to finance and distribute these solutions around the world. Everyone is doing their energetic part and going beyond to be involved, something my human self cannot control. We also had to acknowledge that there would need to be a certain global vibration for the world to be ready for this solution, aligning the visions of multiple collective groups. In this situation, with such new paradigm solutions, it's so much more than visualization—it's an interweaving of situations, people, and their soul evolution. This is why I don't use the word "intention" like something will just magically occur; it has to be in alignment with the highest and best outcome and also in alignment with the soul journey our non-physical self chose before coming into multi-dimensional form.

We recently received large-scale global investor offer, but it's not in the "bank" yet—and I'm sitting here thinking "how the heck can I write about abundance when I look at my bank account right now?" Why? Well, because over the years I feel I have figured out a framework to help us understand what's happening in the world around us, a perspective we can and must hold, and a vision for the future of a new economy and what "business" and "money" will look like. Achieving your tangible desires might have a simple formula. But, bringing into existence something novel, something the world has never seen, can be more like a trek through the jungle. It's a life-transforming experience, and there won't be a well-worn trail.

This perspective that supports my entrepreneurial process started with a cultivation of personal awareness and the requisite spiritual journey. I was fired from a job that wasn't a good fit, but it was the Universe forcing me into a path to transcend and perceive beyond my intellectual mind and catalyze my evolution and personal development. Over this time, I realized that I'm a conscious energetic body, a multi-dimensional being in a human body. I learned that my linear, analytical, reasoning, intellectual, and conscious mind was less than five percent of my decisions and behavior. I discovered that there is an intelligence in my subconscious mind to help me shift unwanted patterns, but more importantly, I had access to a source consciousness, or universal conscious mind that could be available at all times. This source and universal consciousness where mind is connected to everyone and everything, and that I was already part of it—this could be a valuable asset in any business or personal situation.

As someone who always got straight A's, went to schools for the intellectually gifted, and wanted to be the smartest girl in the room, my ego was first frustrated, but then fascinated at the fact that there was a level of intelligence I hadn't reached—and I wanted at It! Sure, this connection to source consciousness supported my heart, peace, and spiritual connection, but once my ego was willing to accept that everything I thought was "intelligence" was so limited, I started out on a quest to research, experience, and apply the source conscious mind to business.

After years of taking programs and classes that were experiential into the vast levels of consciousness we all have access to, I started to realize that I was pretty naturally accessing what we consider to be intuitive intelligence coming from source consciousness. I started receiving information by hearing (clairaudience), sensing and feeling (clairsentience) and just "knowing" (claircognizance). And I was quite on point. When I would meditate, I would have visions. I had to learn how to decipher whether this information originated from my linear mind, a seated fear, or if it was from my higher intelligence. *(Hint: If it comes from fear, or feels contracted, it's not intuition.)*

Intuitive information that comes through from this source connected mind is often neutral and expansive; it "feels right," and you need to practice getting out of your head and into your energy body and to the subtle invisible energy of the everything around you, in order to build your intuitive muscle to help decipher the information. Think about a dolphin: A dolphin uses sonar, energy radiating from its body to the surrounding world, and the energy frequencies detect detailed information their eyes cannot see about what's in their environment, and frequencies return back to their body as information. Humans have the same capabilities; we're just too busy in our head or just don't realize how to use our energy body.

During this time, I was staffing a personal development class and our main teacher asked us to identify our three goals to achieve in the next goal years. Personally, I'm not always gung-ho about goal setting. Although I feel it keeps a structure around our personal or ego wishes, the practice doesn't necessarily support the highest vision of how we are meant to be of service nor our true alignment, which may evolve or transform over time. I believe it's useful to let go of a goal once the higher perspective is shown that it's no longer in alignment or if a different path is shown to be the more aligned path. Anyway, after saying two goals...the third goal which slipped out of my mouth was, "And build the Economy of South America!" I looked behind me in shock, wondering who said that, and then I realized it was me. I didn't know what It meant, and I was flabbergasted! I was thirty-three years old, working for startups in San Francisco. How could I have the audacity to state that I could help build the economy of South America?

After that, the clues kept coming. One by one, by receiving intuitive clues and following them, the next one would appear. To go somewhere, call someone, do something—and every time I did, I got another piece of the puzzle. Energetically, I felt there was a magnetic pull to the countries of Peru and Argentina. I committed to visiting each country for a month. I knew I must be there to help understand what was going on with the economy, especially if I was supposed to help build it!

I became fascinated with the Andean and shamanic approach to cosmology and world view, and, after reading an article about the Andean and Quechua values and how they improved business, I wanted to explore them more. I booked a flight, knowing I would have very little savings when I returned. But I felt I had to do it. After I committed and pulled the trigger, I received a phone call that I would receive back the $50,000 investment, plus interest, that I had made into a company a few years back. Now I had the cushion. I flew to Peru, and the doors flew open. Within two days I happened to be having coffee with the man who wrote the article I read online, a major inspiration for shifting my course. I met powerful business people and entrepreneurs. I did my two weeks of shamanic and Andean quests. During this time, flowers spoke to me saying "move to Lima" and more and more signs from the universe came about. I was living my own business version of The Celestine Prophecy. I didn't feel the same about Argentina when I went there, and knew Peru was where I was meant to be.

When I returned to San Francisco, the intuitive guidance kept coming. I got more clear on what "build the economy of south America" meant to help build a seed capital and entrepreneurial ecosystem so that innovation could improve and entrepreneurship could flourish. At one point, I heard my guidance say to call a friend I hadn't spoken to in years. "Call him, call him" I kept hearing. So I called him up and said, "Hi. I have no idea why I'm calling you, but here's what I know I'm supposed to do in Peru." After our conversation, we realized he had one of the exact things I needed to get me down there to start building projects. No rational or linear mind would have ever known this about him; it was truly my connection to my intuition and source intelligence.

I ended up moving to Lima on my own—just me, a girl with the vision for the country's future and a framework of solutions to help them get there. I wasn't sponsored by a company and had no official title. Everyone thought I was crazy, but I knew my purpose. I continued to use my intuition and my energy body in a country where I didn't speak the language fluently and had never done business before. The three things I was guided to do, all happened in two years—in a developing country, where it could normally take five to ten years.

While in Peru, I had a natural level of trust from my partners and fellow visionaries. We have had many past lives together and had come together with a purpose this time around. I was hired by a powerful international development organization to accomplish one of the goals, and I started my own business. Again, my intuition always was one step ahead of me. On the day we were to launch our product, I was guided to hold back the release, even though we had every logical reason to move as fast as possible. My employee was not happy about the decision, but my advisor and partner trusted my guidance. "You're a witch, Kate. I have seen so much evidence of your ability to understand things others don't and be right on point. It's why I chose to work with you. If you don't want to launch today, then that's fine."

My intuition was right, even though I didn't know what it was. There was something going on behind the scenes that was changing the trajectory of the product.

I got a call two days later about these changes. If we had launched the day we had planned, it would have been chaos for our customers and bad on our brand equity. I would have had to go back to our newly acquired customers and tell them different information. But because I waited, I had mitigated disaster. When we launched with the new changes, we sold out our product in two hours.

I was starting to realize that my full-spectrum intelligence, my multi-dimensional awareness, and my intuitive and connection to source consciousness was my greatest economic, entrepreneurial, and business asset.

*I'm not special; I just learned how to use something
that we all have.*

Since our inherent nature is connected to this intelligence, we just have to remember how to access it after years of working with and worshiping our linear reasoning mind and how to apply it to all aspects of our business and personal life. Your connection to this source intelligence will help you in every aspect: from aligning with the right investors, partners, and clients to coming up with innovations and new economic models, feeling in to what your clients truly want and need, not just what you are selling. I dream of a day when every investor, manager, or boss asks an entrepreneur, potential employee, or potential partner, "What's your connection to source consciousness? Are you able to perceive intelligence you can't see or information that is beyond the books, the numbers, or the meeting?" Because when we take the "woo" out of intuition and source consciousness, and start treating it like it truly is—our natural and most powerful intelligence—and learn how to apply it in tangible situations in business and in life, we can receive the improved alignment, the revealed path, financing, everything...

The trend is already happening in business; meditation, mindfulness, and now emotional intelligence are hot topics and applied in many Fortune 500 companies. Twenty years ago we would have never thought that many Wall Street bankers would be meditating. I see the popularity of meditation and mindfulness as stepping stones of this heightened conscious evolution, and a new business strategy will in fact include heightened consciousness and intuition. It has to. We are at a massive paradigm shift in our economy and we will have to understand things in an upgraded way. In the next twenty to thirty years, our business world and jobs will be affected by automation, self-driving cars, the prevalence of machine learning, and artificial intelligence. Some estimate that up to one-third of the workforce will be displaced by 2035. We're also seeing a massive shift in currency, with the arrival of hundreds of cryptocurrencies and new forms of fundraising. We must know what's coming, and lives will be altered, but I feel there is really no reason to fear. It can be daunting, because, yes, our idea of work and jobs and titles will all change. From a higher perspective, however, we can be assured that it is all happening for a reason; it's part of the linear to multi-dimensional upgrade that humans and business are both experiencing.

We'll have to watch this shift and change with neutrality. We'll have to open our minds and our linear framework to an upgrade. Instead of fear of automation and machine learning, let's think about the possibilities; as the economy shifts to computers doing more of our linear tasks, we can outsource that part of us, the part of us that is linear, limited, and analytical. That will free us to run businesses and create powerful solutions for humanity from our highest-conscious intelligence, instead of using the limited aspect of our mind.

We didn't come to earth to sit at computers and do spreadsheets and emails all day. We came here to expand and create the most amazing solutions, to be in community with each other, and to benefit the souls with whom we share this 3D plane. I think it's great that the analytical part of our world and work will be outsourced, so that we can cultivate and use the most powerful aspect of our humanness—our connection to the universal and source conscious mind. When we connect to that, we are instantly in tune with the appropriate framework for the highest and best outcome for our human family and all involved. Yes, the workforce shift will create an existential crisis for many people, especially in the United States where we are deeply defined by our job, our title, our income, and our industry. We let it rule our identity. It's why we ask each other, "What do you do?" When this massive abruption occurs, our friends and family will be forced to go inward, to explore the version of themselves that is not identified by their work or their title. It will be another big step in our human conscious evolution.

We will need to be compassionate and help others in their quest for their true identity, their divine nature, and the purpose of their soul's evolution, not their job or title. Because of this, I believe we all chose to be here at this time, at this major inflection point in human history. With change, there will be pain and perceived loss of financial stability and power. We must keep the higher perspective and facilitate the continued evolution, supporting others in their growth and remaining in neutrality. There truly is a new world on the other side, and I believe that as the linear and hierarchical foundations continue to dissolve, we will enter into a new era of community, potential, and harmony...if we so choose.

This is why I am also very excited about cryptocurrency and the underlying technology of blockchain. Cryptocurrency, although often misunderstood and misused as a new money-making entity, did not begin with that in mind. It was designed to provide more self-sovereignty and limit reliance on central banks and those that control market forces and the movement of "money." It is taking our linear concept of money and making it multi-dimensional, through a distributed and decentralized system with more freedom for the average person. Really, at the end of the day—money, our currency, the U.S. dollar is simply a belief, an energy, and a consciousness. Money has power because we believe it does. In fact, if you looked at the truth behind the U.S. dollar, there really is very little value to it. But we believe it has value.

Cryptocurrency is allowing us to monetize and bring value to other types of values, concepts, work, and ideals. Coins already exist as incentives for someone to generate renewable energy, work in collaboration, or even participate in positive behavior. Now that these "incentives" will be able turned into a token and exchanged into the "dollars" that pay our bills, we will enter a new era of abundance. You'll pay for your lunch with the solar coin you generated from your house, for example. Teenage girls in Afghanistan are doing computer coding and being paid in cryptocurrency, where their country does not allow them to have a bank account or access income-generating opportunities. Women farmers in Sub-Saharan Africa are getting loans and financial inclusion opportunities where they have never before.

The underlying technology of blockchain will be a powerful tool in helping the 2.5 billion who are unbanked access and participate in the global economy, and that benefits us all. Women who are pregnant in a developing country can receive a token for getting prenatal checkups to improve the well-being of their child, tokens which she can use in a local store to buy food while simultaneously supporting public health initiatives. Children around the world will be incentivized by tokens to upcycle waste into something that is valuable for our planet and food supply. We will shift into receiving micro-transactions for watching an advertisement or a YouTube video, instead of the other way around. You will be able to own our digital footprint and your identity, and if others want access, they will have to pay you, instead of the other way around—where everyone makes money off your digital footprint except you.

This is the continued experience of shifting into multiple streams of income, transactions where abundance will occur in ways we never thought possible. We will be able to transact with limited fees and save money in purchases and transfers. The sharing economy will become a true "sharing of wealth." Rather than a portal like Uber or Airbnb that controls the centralized platform and is worth billions of dollars as a centralized company, we will be able to transact, ride, buy, or rent peer to peer with trust and safety without needing to pay a large fee. It will take some time, but again, it's all part of this multi-dimensional shift into what our experience of money, business, the economy, and our ultimate evolution are to become.

So stay neutral as you observe the shifts. Keep strong, be in faith, and stay connected to your highest-conscious intelligence. Use it as you most powerful economic and financial aspect. Watch this play out. Get out of your head and let your linear mind take a back seat with your intuition taking the wheel. Trust your intuition and connection to source consciousness and watch the magic unfold.

Kate Mulder is a speaker, entrepreneur, and futurist who has been recognized by the World Economic Forum and international media outlets for her pioneering approaches to economic development, impact strategies, and unique perspective on the role of human conscious evolution with blockchain, AI, and economic thinking. With experience as a global entrepreneur, seed investor, strategic specialist, executive coach, speaker, and facilitator, Kate's passion is making the 'cutting-edge' a reality. Kate has served as special advisor to the Inter-American Development Bank to help build a seed capital ecosystem in LATAM, spearheaded the Center for Global Entrepreneurship, and has driven business development and strategy for numerous tech-startups and social impact companies. Kate also has 10 years of specialized training in human behavior, energy psychology, intuitive development, and human conscious evolution. Often called the "Real life Wendy Rhoades," she has worked with business and finance executives, investors, and entrepreneurs around the globe to maximize their optimal functioning, quantum intelligence, intuition, and higher conscious awareness. She believes our human conscious evolution with new business strategies will enable the future of a thriving global economic framework.

Kate is currently the co-founder of Neusis Global, a company dedicated enabling the future of regenerative, profitable economies using new paradigm holistic ecosystems that generate pure food and pure water. Additional clients, projects, and speaking appearances include; The United Nations, The World Economic Forum, JP Morgan, Net Impact, BlackRock, The Feminine Intelligence, The Kauffman Foundation, Women Investing In Women, The Next Web, Draper University, New Economic Thinking Institute, Startup Weekend, and Stanford University.

Information or speaking inquiries: **www.mulderkate.com**
Work with Kate one-on-one: **www.mulderkate.com/work-with-kate**

Into the Arms of Abundance

BY ALEXANDRA PALLAS

ABUNDANTIA

Behold the Goddess Abundantia. Just birthed from the womb of the earth, creamy skin spotted with patches of still-wet mud, wrapped in her mother's embrace.

In these very first moments, she already knows who she is. No quivering wail, no jittery squeal.

***

Mama's elixir: the milk of the starry sky from grandmother moon (ah, generations); blessed honey from the queen of the hive; the oil of pink lotus from the ancient ones.

From this maternal nurturance, Abundantia learns the medicine of a fully open heart.

***

Her tiny arms flail around; she has no control. She is the embraced one, not yet the embracer.

***

She has no control.

WHEN THE UNIVERSE SPEAKS

A Hook Sinks In (and It Hurts)

"Bring three stones that represent three 'hooks' in your life— three nagging, core issues that you just cannot not seem to shake off, that are clearly getting in the way your personal, emotional, and professional well-being."

These were the instructions sent to me in preparation for my first shamanic energy medicine retreat. I arrived at the hot summer desert retreat center in Joshua Tree National Park with three stones in hand, one of which was a polished unakite wand. It was stunning, with greens and pinks swirling and flecks of glitter glistening. I was mesmerized by it. And, I conveniently avoided identifying my three hooks, focusing instead on feeling both eagerly excited about the retreat and guilty about how much money I had spent on the unakite wand.

The time came for working with a retreat partner on our hooks. It was my turn to identify my first hook and select a stone to work with from among the three. "Money" came to me right way. I felt strangled by my relationship with money: fear of spending and fear of saving turning into overspending in denial, followed by guilt, shame, avoidance, and then more fear. I chose a stone with my eyes closed...the unakite wand landed in my fingers. I chuckled at the irony of selecting the stone that I felt guilty about spending money on.

After a full, gut-wrenching, and emotionally draining (yet very healing) day of energetically working on my "money hook," I was to put my stone into the bonfire—turning it into a kuya, or mystical healing stone. It was beautiful concept in the tradition of the Q'ero Inkan shaman of Peru—that we could turn our greatest wounds into our greatest healing tools. And it was a majestic fire ceremony, chanting under the full moon. I was feeling very proud of myself for the work I did in clearing my money issues.

But the real initiation was yet to begin.

Ritual Burial Knocks (and Fine, I'll Answer)

Later that night, I heard a little voice whispering to me something I did not at all want to hear: "Bury the unakite wand in the desert."

I ignored it; it was utterly ridiculous. Bury the stone I just turned into a magical healing tool? Why on earth would I do that? The stone was expensive. I had already done the spiritual processing work. The stone had already been through the fire. I was not simply going to throw this pricey, powerful, beautiful healing wand out into the sand because some little voice in my head said so.

But the more I pushed back, the louder the voice grew: "You must bury this stone in the desert."

Damn it. I took a breath and caved in to what I already knew, deep inside: If I couldn't do this—get over my fear of burying my most expensive stone—I had not truly alchemized my work regarding money. I saw that the act of listening to my instincts (no matter how much my mind couldn't understand them) was somehow part of my recovery from this core money wound in me. That life's biggest lessons could not be planned and sometimes occur "off script"—in this case, for me, *after* the formal fire ceremony. So in the dark, I went out to a very random, unidentifiable spot in the desert, and I buried the stone in the symbolic ritual of burying this toxic relationship I had with money. I cried...first because I didn't want to give up the stone, and then because I was ashamed about that, and finally in frustration that it had been so difficult for me to simply follow the voice in my heart without being so worried about outcomes. It was cathartic.

But the Universe was just getting started with me.

The Claws Come Out (and the Universe Speaks)

Fall came. I went back again for another week-long shamanic studies retreat. Then winter came, and I returned. And finally, during my fourth retreat about a year and a half later, sitting in the same retreat center at Joshua Tree, something called within me. It was an itch I couldn't scratch...I found myself distracted, being magnetically pulled outside into the open desert. Finally, I realized—*it was my unakite wand calling me back.*

I charged off into the desert in the general direction of where I thought I had maybe buried my wand, almost two years before. I dug and dug and turned up sand, ripping out small plants...until finally, my mind won. I had hoped to avoid the rational thought of "I will never be able to find that stone out here. It's impossible!" But my mind was right: There was no way I'd be able to find it.

And then I noticed:

"I."

Aha.

"I"...echoing in my mind.

There is no way "I" would be able to find my stone.

I looked around me at the earth I dug up. I was sick to my stomach at the sight of my own entitlement. It was as if I was a mad woman, clawing up the earth with my fingernails without so much as a "please" or a "thank you." Again, I cried...I was ashamed, like I had literally scratched up someone's face in a maniacal fury of my own me-ness. I crawled to a shaded spot and sat silently for quite some time. I suddenly felt something new—I was extraordinarily connected to the spirit of the mother in the earth itself. Outside of the mystery teachings of the Q'ero. Outside of the retreat agenda. Just within myself.

"I am so sorry," I proclaimed aloud. "Please forgive me. I thought I heard the voice of my stone asking to be returned to me. If it's in the highest good for me to have it back, would you please place my hand over my stone?"

I raised my hand in the air. Through no effort of my own, my hand was physically moved and thrust down right next to me.

I wiggled my hand into the warm sand, slowly and gently...

...and found my fingers wrapped around my unakite wand.

ABUNDANTIA

Behold the Goddess Abundantia. She who holds the chalice of cascading overflow. She who offers the eternal cornucopia. She who is the seed, the stalk, the fruit, and the flower...the sun, the rain, and the earth.

***

She pours from her bottomless cup...a potion of sweet nectar, geranium oil, stardust, and raindrops...over my head, in anointing. Slowly from my crown in endless flow, spreading in all directions to drip down the back of my neck, over my ears, and across my forehead into my eyes...mixing with my own sweat and tears.

Finally making its way onto my lips.
I have waited so long for this.

***

"Where have you been?" I ask her.
She laughs.
"My friend," she whispers. "I have always been here."

OUT OF SPIRITUAL DEBT AND INTO PRIVILEGED PROSPERITY

Since that time in the desert, my financial situation has substantially "worsened."

I have *massive* debt.

And it's in part due to the fact that I have not always earned or spent money—as energetic currency—in a way that is a reflection of and in alignment with my soul's highest purpose. I have, in many cases, not clearly defined what it is I truly want for myself and the world. I have misdirected and misplaced this energetic currency as some of my life choices have been misdirected and misplaced. Examples:

Moving frequently in my younger years (costly) in avoidance of self (But "wherever you go, there you are!")

Starting (and in many cases, not finishing) pricey higher education or certificate programs that were not in alignment with my soul's purpose

Binge spending on trips or experiences before sitting in the truth of what is in the higher good

Taking day jobs that, while lucrative, have not fulfilled my real purpose

But while my financial situation has "worsened," my relationship with money has improved tremendously.

I got what I asked for, out there in the desert: *a healed relationship with money.* I never asked to be debt-free. I asked to be healed of my money wound. And that's what I got.

I have said "yes" to life more than "no," and I have a feeling I won't ever regret that.

Where my financial debt has been a reflection of my spiritual debt, I have taken a long, hard look in the mirror—and made some big shifts in order to come into greater alignment with who I really am. This has been a gift.

I am not afraid to exchange energetic currency on the things that are part of my soul's purpose.

I have practiced gratitude for my main sources of income, which have grown to be in greater alignment with my soul's purpose.

But it cannot be overlooked that the primary enabler for all of this can be summed up in one word: *privilege.* I have been privileged in my race, in my upbringing, and in my family support (luck; not earned). My relationship to the concepts of debt, abundance, and prosperity are inherently defined by my privilege. This means that my entire mythical life story is not one of empowered manifestation through "mystical work" (although, I do believe there is partial truth to this notion) but one of beginning with a baseline of privilege. The most powerful spiritual debt I have only just recently begun to repay is the one of dismantling my blindness to my own privilege and how this fits into my preconceived ideas about spirituality, manifesting abundance, and what prosperity is and who it serves and should serve.

ABUNDANTIA

Behold the Goddess Abundantia. Naked in her thousand rose-petaled crown and her jeweled slippers.

Carefree, she dances with a gentle breeze, dances in a hurricane, dances through the flames, dances submerged. She dances always.

"Can I join you?" I ask her.

She doesn't hear me. She doesn't see me. I wear the blindfold of turning away from the world, from my own my own true self, and my own real purpose. And so I am invisible to her.

***

Do you want to dance? Do you want her undivided attention? Better get started in knowing who you really are, and why you're

*really here. Your wants are invisible to her. She trades only in
truth. Come back when you're ready to get real.*

***

*Slowly, I take off my clothes. This is me. In all my years of shame.
Witnessing all their years of pain. Burned at the stake. Or taken.*

*I peel off my masks. From yesterday. From when I was thirty-one.
And twenty-two. And seventeen. And eight. And two. And long,
long before that.*

Abundantia, here I am. See me. Hear me. Here I am.

***

She turns to behold me:

"You, my sister," she whispers, "are forgiven."

WANTING FOR NOTHING

The Universe Abandons Me (Or So I Think)

Over the past ten years: I have experienced the honor and joys of being a mama; I moved back East and repaired my relationship with my mother; I have made new friends, true soul sisters; I bought a house and have turned it into a home; and I have integrated my soulful life's purpose into my career.

And I got pregnant by someone I barely knew, and struggled to cope, alone, with hyperemesis gravidarum (constant, severe nausea and vomiting) for seven months of my pregnancy; I survived massive, long-term, clinical sleep deprivation while caring for a chronically ill infant/toddler/small child, alone; I have battled addictive tendencies; I lost two pregnancies in a short amount of time; and I was hospitalized for a month for extreme chronic fatigue syndrome.

I return again to how my personal wounds have been embedded within my privilege. See, along the way, I gave up on the Universe. Sole parenting and health challenges made me feel I could not possibly get much lower, and the Universe I was once awakened to trust and obey had disappeared. Everything I knew to be true as part of my previous spiritual experiences was no longer real because I had endured pain and could not accept that pain as part of my spiritual experience. This feeling churned and alchemized into a potent poison of wanting, resentment, and self-pity.

I distracted myself. I stopped listening to my intuition. I stopped feeling grateful. I stop putting things into perspective. I simply got through each day.

A Miraculous Reminder of the Power of Gratitude

Being the sole caretaker of a chronically ill baby who became a chronically ill toddler prevented me from having the personal time or space to open up to romantic love in a healthy way for many years. The loneliness I felt was at times intolerable.

Then, several years ago, I found myself sitting in a cafe, watching all the "happy families" go by. On this day, I noticed that my reactions of jealousy or judgment or anger to watching these "others" who "had it all" had disappeared and that I felt truly open and grateful not only for all I had but in the faith that I would find love again. So, out loud in the middle of the cafe, I said, "I'm ready." And in my mind's eye, I created an image of him: a kind yet feisty, strong and beefy, funny, health and wellness-oriented single father. Thirty seconds later, a man sat down and introduced himself to me. *He was a kind yet feisty, strong and beefy, funny, health and wellness-oriented single father!*

It was a wake-up call reminder that when we operate from a place of gratitude, miracles are possible. I realized that I had broken my pattern of blame, shame, and suffering and taken responsibility for how I allowed my perception to drive my reality. At the time, I was more grateful for remembering that miracles are possible than that this sexy fella had sat down next to me. I knew that my relationship with Universe was the most important relationship I would ever have. And I knew I had done nothing to deserve or not deserve this miracle.

But when he asked me out, I froze. And when we finally got together and became friends, I froze again. And I stayed frozen.

My relationship with the Universe had reignited, but I realized that I was in trauma recovery from a relationship I never even really knew I had.

The Goddess Rises Within Me

Because of the series of fires I had walked through—pregnancy, birth, pregnancy loss, sole parenting, severe illness, emotional trauma—I had unwittingly developed a subconscious belief system that *following my heart was no longer safe*. It was not just that I felt abandoned by this thing called "the Universe"; it was that I had felt betrayed by "*Her*"—by the Pachamama, the Earth itself, the Gaia Mother who was supposed to unconditionally guide and hold me. Where was *She* when I needed her? When I was pregnant alone, birthing alone, mothering alone, and too sick to stand up for the better part of a year? I had lost my connection to her, and in that I lost my connection to abundance—my ability to commune with the divine feminine energy that holds, supports, and supplies us with unconditional love.

Then I remembered my time in the desert.

I realized it was She who I clawed at, in the sand—and who forgave me for it. She who extended me grace and led my hand to my hidden unakite wand. She who gave me breath as I pushed my daughter's tiny body out of my own. She who offered me exactly what I had asked for, even when I couldn't admit that it was me who asked for it. She who delivered the sexy fella to me through miraculous manifestation. And, yes, She by whom I felt betrayed.

She flooded back into me: my cellular memory, my nourished senses, my cracking open heart, my butterfly wings opening. I realized that She had always been there within me; it was me who had turned away from Her. I began to forgive Her through forgiving myself in years of hidden shames: both my entitlement and my self-abandonment.

But, who is *She*?

She is the fierce warrior on the mountain of truth. The sovereign queen. The teary-eyed little girl who is softly held. The nurturing mother who embraces and protects. The witch in the woods who brews. The mermaid in the sacred indigo waters. The sorceress in the night. The winged angel above. She is the smile of compassion. The hands of *abundance*—the source of unconditional love that beats across all time and space. She is all of the faces of the goddess begging to be expressed through me *to stand for a higher good for all.*

And I remembered Her through the portal of my own truth.

(P.S. I married him.)

ABUNDANTIA

*Behold the Goddess Abundantia. Shriveled and wrinkled in
a tattered blanket of time-space. One foot here, one foot not-here.
One foot now, one foot not-now. Oh, the ever-slowing gait...
the hooded eyes...the skin and bones...the crackling sound of this
reality breaking into small bits around her; yet knows she has it
all. She has always had it all.*

***

*She rides on a magic carpet in the night and takes anyone
who asks along for a ride. There is no fare, no rite of passage;
through her heart, she alchemizes moonlight into pure love and
shares with all. She is a giver.*

She cackles in the winds, "Yaooooooh, you can tooooo!"

***

*We watch from below as she, a shooting star, flies through the
midnight sky.*

*We are here now. We are all the gatekeepers of her house. We
are all the makers of her medicine. We are all the farmers of her
fruits. We are all the dancers of her dance.*

***

"My daughters!" she signals through the ethers, "Rise!"

In the quest to uncover the planet's most ancient and mysterious wisdom teachings, I found only the shattered and scattered artifacts of my own soul. Collecting myself, piece by piece, I became whole again: a stained-glass-window looking through itself; a priestess of the temple of the senses; a sorceress of the jungle of life; a sister of sisters; a mother of babes; an enchantress of life and death.

Alexandra Pallas is a divine feminine activist, integrative mystical therapy practitioner, mindful education advocate, instructional designer of sacred learning, and modern day priestess. She has an unwavering curiosity and sense of adventure for learning about and honoring ancient wisdom teachings so that we may collectively remember our truest nature as spirit embodied. She has studied multiple lineages, and weaves a tapestry of age-old traditions and modern magic into her work.

Alexandra offers private sessions and in-person/online devotional journeys—birthed from her greatest wounds and shadows—as empowerment portals of self-realization, self-healing, and spiritual awakening. Journey with Alexandra at **www.apallas.com.**

Fluidity and Abundance

BY GAVIN PAULEY

Abundance is not something that can be materialized in the world—not in money, possessions, or even life experiences. It must be discovered deep in the consciousness.

The key is to dissect the different dimension of causal thought patterns that exists within ourselves, and strive to embody a life experience that speaks to our soul and enriches the way we interact with other people and the physical world that surrounds us. Each of us has to let our unique and constantly evolving value system guide our lives toward abundance and prosperity.

Abundance grows as we expand human connections
and find passion and purpose in alignment with personal
values and in balance with the various aspects of who
were are as individuals.

This is the richness of life.

EXPANDING CONNECTIONS

I love to connect with people. New conversations expand my mind and help me focus my perspective of the world to be more in tune with what I actually value. Over the course of my journey to meet new people and have new conversations, I am often faced with the same question, "What do you do?"

This question dominates the way people interact and value each other socially. For many of us, our mind immediately jumps to work, as if work is our only purpose and is the only way others can understand us and value us. The question "What do you do?" is very limiting and infers that we only do one thing or only have one purpose in life. When using this question as a jumping off point to get to know a person, we reinforce the limited way that people come to understand one another's values and the purpose that we carry.

But now it's time to upturn this value system, and it's deceivingly simple! We need to reinvent the way that we interact with other people and the questions we ask to get to know them.

My value system for conversations and people was reinvented when a new soul asked me, "What are your passions?" She then clarified, "Or passion?" I closed my eyes as I do when I am surprised by a good question and need to look within for answers. I indeed have many passions. I indeed accomplish many tasks over the course of my day. I do many things. However, I thought to myself: "Is one more important than the other?"

My mind was calmed by the remembrance that all we must do in life is exist. For me, existence is about realizing that there is a greater purpose out there. We are only fleeting manifestations of energy that must exist and observe the day to day. We must observe our experience and notice common patterns of thought that arise in our minds and come to peace with the fact that perhaps we cannot change anything. We must be fully alive and take small steps to support the existence of those around us, easing their suffering along the way.

PASSION AND PURPOSE

When my friend asked me, "What are your passions? Or passion?" I realized that a material- and action-based value system dominates human interactions and the importance we hold for one another. We compare ourselves to each other, what we do in life, and what we have materialized. We even compare our passions.

Many of us believe we must become more and more efficient and effective in the day to day to have more passions—so much so that we end up forcing it. Instead, we need to prioritize and decide that one thing may be more important than the other. While prioritization may help us schedule our days and holds value for just getting things done, we shouldn't become overly dependent upon a comparison-based value system. Even if we must prioritize eight hours a day while at work, we needn't become obsessed with comparison and the hierarchy of our rank.

A technique I use to detach myself from time and instead focus on prioritizing my daily responsibilities is discovering a unity of purpose. I start to notice common patterns in thoughts that I have—what makes me feel good, people with whom I enjoy working, and materials I like to work with. My intention is to find the common threads between my thoughts, my feelings, the people that I am connected with, the passions that we share, and the things that we do into a woven tapestry of truth.

In my life, releasing patterns of self-judgment and judgment towards others has led to deeper connection with more souls. I learn from each person I meet and connect the purpose behind the many things that I work with. I aim to exist harmoniously with the energy that surrounds me.

After turning inward to understand my thoughts, feelings, and values and how they influence my connections, my passions, and my work, I found my answer. What is my passion? The answer is one word and continues to be the unifying theme for my purpose: *water.*

With that, my soul began to frame my life purpose as being a protector of water. (This is not to say that my efforts will ever compare *whatsoever* to the long and historical fight of Native peoples for the right to their own water—a resource they have maintained sustainably and protected as an ancient wisdom for eons.) I am a different kind of water protector. I am white and I have privilege.

PERSONAL VALUES

I am grateful for the privilege I have in my fight to protect water. Unlike indigenous communities' fight, I am not risking my life. My water resources are not in jeopardy. I have not experienced the persisting and historical atrocities of having my rights and resources stolen from me. My mind is not completely overwhelmed with worry about the future of my people and my culture. I am not worried for the health of my children. My connection to the issue is nothing that can be compared to the Native fight, and there is nothing I can say or do to encapsulate the Native experience or relate to it. All I can do is try my best to understand it.

I feel constrained by the unique privilege of public service, and have had to learn to protect water through the imminent constraints of static regulations. I've been able to move beyond this value system by expanding my purpose, working beyond the system that contains me, and now have connected myself to nonprofit and independent water projects. I've expanded my work to move beyond the system to fit my purpose. But first I had to understand the purpose behind my work. Traditional water regulation is problem-focused. It focuses on issues with water, such as contamination. It simply makes sure people are not drinking bad water.

While a focus on issues and problems may be the predominant methodology used by the system I work within, I do not value that system. Even though it is the basis of my work and it supports me, my knowledge base, and my purpose, it does not have to be my guiding force. I value solutions most. I am a *solutionary*.

Solutionary is a new word for me. I use it. I talk about it. And I spread it. It is about using a new lens to look at the world...a new perspective. It acknowledges and recognizes the importance in all historical fights on social, economic, and environmental justice. It respects that those fights are far from over. However, it suggests a focus on solution-based methodologies and a drive for progress.

In my journey to become a solutionary and live my purpose—and thus magnetize abundance in my life—I am constantly redefining my own value system. I accept that it is different and I learn to support it through my mental patterns, diversity in my work, and living life as the truest version of myself. For me, as a queer human, this has been a beautiful and ongoing journey since I was a toddler.

BALANCING MASCULINITY WITH FEMININITY

In a recent conversation with my mother, I realized the iterative and constantly unfolding nature of my masculine and feminine energies and the inherent fact they will never fit the same mold as the check boxes outlined and managed by the bureaucracy—and will never be in balance with the patriarchal value system in power.

The conversation reminded me of a struggle between the masculine and feminine that haunted me from my youth through to my adolescence. It was a concept kids inevitably could not let go of: Gavin—as a little boy—liked to wear dresses and dress up the same way a girl would. Though this was a source of shame for me, it was also a way to connect with my mother and explore my divine feminine. In school when I would feel the burn of kids recounting a story of my mother and I, both in dresses, high-heels, and earrings, standing together in line in Starbucks, I would return to my mother for her consolation and nurturing energy. These were just the first bashes to my little boy sense of masculinity, however, throughout my life there continue to be situations where I do not fit the mold of the traditionally masculine man.

In the recent conversation with my mother I was enlightened to a new story—a new understanding of the internal conflict my little self was going through. As a little boy I would intently look at my penis and say that I didn't want that there. I was so uncomfortable with my body, how to express my masculinity, and how to connect to other boys that I didn't want to be in a boy's body anymore.

I searched for more, and in the end I found acceptance within and found a balance between the masculine and the feminine energies inside of me. Throughout my adolescence, I had a convoluted connection to both genders. I had an intense and deep confusion about my own identity, what gender meant to me, how I was supposed to express it, and how I was supposed to relate to the masculine and feminine socially and sexually. Were my best friends supposed to be boys or girls? Why was I supposed to flirt with girls when I was attracted to boys?

Today I can confidently look at my penis and say I love my body and all the magical experiences it guides me through. My male body is beautiful in its capacity to be a vessel that carries me through a mountain pass to a pristine spring, to be the drum that is erotically beaten by a masculine energy, or to be the stand for my brain that can think!

The acceptance of my body did not arise from just anywhere. Masculine confidence could not forcibly make me like the way I looked and how I interacted with other people. The acceptance of myself and the manifestation I have taken in this life came from accepting human connection in whatever form it may take. It came from deconstructing my masculinity, fostering a nurturing energy, and learning to value people in a new way. It came from recognizing the beauty inside myself and led to the realization that I must appreciate my own imperfection in order to start relating to others.

I can recall a pivotal change in mental pattern for me that started to deconstruct my resentment toward masculinity and the traditional man. As a queer human, I have always been confused by boxes on forms. I am never sure. Do I check the M for male box? The F for female box? Or somewhere in between? Even for medical and educational forms, do I check the gay box or the bisexual box? Do these boxes do my identity justice? I will not break my gender or sexuality down in terms of the same boxes supported by a patriarchal value system. I will not check the M box. I will not check the F box. Is sexual orientation really a box? Are the complex systems in my mind and sexual body simply a box? I don't think so.

DEFINING SEXUALITY AND GENDER EXPRESSION

I define my sexuality as falling along a spectrum, just like my gender expression. I am not quite masculine and I am not quite feminine. My sexuality falls along the bisexual spectrum with an intimate understanding that I am much closer to the gay side.

Along my bisexual spectrum there exists the ever impending opportunity I may shift for a given moment of time as I admire a beautiful woman. However, the fluidity of the spectrum is grounded by my identification as homo-romantic.

For me, homo-romantic means I quickly shift back to my familiar side of the spectrum returning to the gays. In other words, my romantic partners are men. The exploration shifting to the "other side" reveals the fluidity and opportunity that exists within us all—the opportunity to love. To love another human for their essence—with nothing but an open heart. The other side is not dark or light. But the empowerment of shifting from one to the other is enlightening. I feel empowered as I explore emerging language and techniques to define my sexuality in ways I had never thought of before.

Coming to terms with a more fluid sexuality and being open to a myriad of connections went hand in hand with valuing men and women in a more wholesome way. I can look back on these experiences, now, with confident vulnerability. With a sense of my masculinity and an acceptance of my femininity. With a confidence entering into the world and the foresight to enter into it intentionally.

A NEW VALUE SYSTEM IN THE EXISTING WORLD

The world right now is existing in a state of disarray. An intense flux of masculinity is at work. Swirling energies of the patriarchy are breaking down our sense of our rights, breaking down the way that we interact with the world. If they continue to alter our value system enough, they will define which resources hold value. Let's define our own value system that affords us a sustainable future of environmental harmony, social equity, economic freedom, and an abundant life.

When we define our value systems we must do so in a way that is true to ourselves and the way we interact with and value other people. We must to so in a way that respects the environment and values and protects resources in a solutionary way. We can then look back on our pain and suffering with confident vulnerability and move forward. In this way, we discover flow and experience love, joy, and abundance. We will become change-makers and will begin to value the well-being of other people and our planet over ourselves. This change in mindset will help protect earth's resources, including water as the heart of all of her resources. The water cycle will move us toward balance and help us to stay in a flow with abundance and prosperity. It will dissolve what is not love and inclusion. It will teach us about abundance. Water is the essence of who we are! Water must be in balance just as the masculine and feminine must be in balance.

Through the vibration of love and prosperity, we can explore new connections and begin to galvanize to create the change we wish to see in the world. Change starts in very minimal ways. Instead of asking, "What do you do?" Ask, "What are your passions? Or passion?" Instead of the typical, "How are you doing?" try asking, "How are you feeling?" We must reinvent the way people interact. We must tune in to each other's energies. We must define our own value system. And we must be in balance with our watery planet in order to fully receive the abundance and prosperity that is all around us.

Gavin Pauley works as an environmentalist, partnering with both government and nonprofit agencies. Gavin is a queer human in the ongoing process of figuring out how to fit into the system. Connect with Gavin on Instagram at **alwaysgavinagoodtime.**

True Financial Freedom

BY CORA POAGE

Do you desire financial freedom?

Who doesn't?

Do you think financial freedom has anything to do with how much money you make or owe?

It doesn't.

Are you staring at this page wide-eyed and flabbergasted?

Good.

Because I am about to *blow your mind.*

And set you free.

If Freedom is what you truly want...and if you close your eyes, connect with your heart, and listen, I have a feeling you will hear your call for freedom.

I know it's what I would love. And most of the time, I feel free. No matter what number is in my bank account. Or on credit cards. Or owed in taxes.

One of the sneakiest ways to stay asleep, limited, or "stuck in the Matrix," if you will, is to give our power away to money. Because then, on some level, we are always a slave to a wild goose chase illusion that keeps us out of the moment (where true peace and freedom reside) and in the past or future, worrying about finances.

Here are some examples of this trick:

When I have such-and-such amount in savings, then I will relax.
When I pay off all my debt, then I will feel free.
When I finally hit that income goal, then I will be truly abundant.

Or the insidious...

I will enjoy my life once I am retired and living off my savings.

How about this re-frame?

Let's *choose* to feel peace, freedom, and abundance *now*. Let's relax and enjoy our lives *now*.

If I can do it, *anyone* can do it.

Yet, it has taken years of healing around my old money story, much of it based on my childhood and societal conditioning.

At a very young age, I began to give money *a lot* of power. I decided that it would determine the happiness, success, and even survival of myself and my family. I equated lack of money with pain, marriages ending, and suffering. I connected an excess of money with love, families staying together, and peace.

There are many reasons for this.

My parents divorced when I was three, and I saw both of them struggle financially. I knew money was tight; in fact, when I was very young, I started to feel like I was a burden, another mouth to feed and body to clothe. My parents never said this. In fact, they assured me of the opposite. But I drew my own conclusions.

I told myself I would *never* be a burden on anyone, if I could help it.

When I was six years old I stumbled upon the traumatic information that the elusive Santa Claus didn't exist (sorry if I am bursting anyone's bubble here). I made the connection that instead of a round-bearded magical man, my beautiful parents were filling Santa's shoes and playing the role of

Ol' St. Nick. That year, I was spending Christmas at my father's house and I was aware that he didn't have much extra money, if any. I knew we were, by American standards, rather poor. I was devastated by the thought of my father struggling to put Christmas together for me.

With deep devotion, I saved my McDonald's Happy Meal toys for the months leading up to December 25. I still remember the look on my father's face as he came down the stairs Christmas morning to see his first-grade daughter filling the holiday stockings with small plastic toys from a shoe box. Talk about over-responsibility and allowing my fear around money to take away my power, pleasure, and enjoyment of life, even as a young child. I let my money beliefs overrun the joy of Christmas!

When we visited various offices to pay utility bills and such, I put my hands over my ears and hummed. I didn't want to hear how much we were spending that I felt we didn't have to spend. Money, or the lack of it, began to scare me. More and more and more.

I was taught (maybe at church, maybe at home or both) that rich people were greedy, so when we did have money, we seemed to always give it away. I registered this as the "right" thing to do.

I didn't realize the immense power I had given money to determine my well-being until three years ago when I was on the phone for a session with my mentor.

"Kirra, I feel crazy around money," I admitted. "I look at my income and I feel successful, and I look at my debt and I feel like a total failure. What gives?"

As we talked, we realized that I was on a roller coaster of judgment around money and the only way I could take my power back and feel peace was to stop connecting my life success or failure to my finances.

It was a game that I couldn't win. The roller coaster would continue indefinitely. Good/bad, right/wrong, success/failure...all based on numbers. Furthermore, one of my deepest darkest fears around money was that I was destined to mess up and live a life of lack anyways. No matter how financially savvy, informed, or skilled I became, I carried an energy of dread and foreboding. There was only one choice that would lead me to true financial freedom. I had to choose to feel free, worthy, safe, successful, more than okay as is, no matter what was in my account or on my credit cards.

"Are you ready for this?" she asked. "You know once you commit to taking your power back around money, you are going to create an opportunity to actually do so. Maybe a major one."

"I am ready," I said, with only a slight wavering of my voice. Gulp.

Two days later, I received a call from my accountant.

"So Cora, I am not sure how this happened—"

I waited.

"But you and Ben owe about $25,000 dollars *more* in taxes than we had estimated this year. I am so sorry for the oversight."

He explained further, but I didn't hear a word. His voice sounded muffled.

My heart sank. My body went into shock and panic mode. My monkey mind took over...

We have to move to a place with lower rent.
I have to quit the gym.
I need to take on twice as many clients.
No more travel for a long time.
Everything must change.

And the judgments...

I am a failure.
This is all my fault.
I knew this would happen.
I am not good with money.

My life is going to fall apart.
Ben will hate me.
I'm going to die. (Hey, the ego/fear voice doesn't have to be rational.)

It was a massive freak out moment.

My good friend Orion has a brilliant example for when the ego and fear take over. He says that the Ego starts screaming "THE BOAT IS SINKING! THE BOAT IS SINKING! EVERYONE'S GOING TO DIE!!!"

Meanwhile his friends are looking at him, perplexed and saying, "Dude, Orion, there is NO boat."

Well, I definitely felt like I was on the Titanic and we were going down.

And then I remembered Kirra's voice.

"Are you ready for this? You know once you commit to taking your power back around money, you are going to create an actual opportunity to do so. Maybe a major one."

"Shit, here it is." I thought to myself. "This is the opportunity to take my power back."

So, after a few *very* deep breaths, I sat down, and asked myself, "How am I going to *choose* to relate to this?"

I realized that this was the moment, *my* moment. This was my opportunity to truly take my power back from money in real time. I imagined little me filling the stockings, covering her ears at bill time, and feeling more and more fear around money.

I decided to nurture her and parent her a bit, speaking out loud to my little one, the one who had begun to make all the fearful connections to money.

I closed my eyes, dropped into my heart, and imagined myself kneeling next to six-year-old me.

Babe, Coco, you are so sweet and strong and generous. I know that money scares you right now and that's okay, but just know that you are more powerful than the money. And it's here on earth for us to play and explore with it, rather than be scared of it. You can see it like the Monopoly money, I know you love being banker. Let's decide that money is safe and that there is more than enough for everyone. How does that feel love, better? Let's choose to have fun with the money game, yes? And please know that you are always supported, loved, held, and that you are never a burden. You are the opposite of a burden. You are a limitless gift to the world, always. I love you.

Once little me felt a bit more at ease, I shifted into self-forgiveness around the main limiting beliefs around money.

I forgive myself for buying into the misunderstanding that money is hard to manage and create.

I forgive myself for judging myself and my family as bad with money.

I forgive myself for buying into the misunderstanding that my worth, value, success, survival, and lovability is dependent on money.

I forgive myself for believing that lack of money means lack of love or families breaking up.

I forgive myself for judging myself as a burden.

Big deep breath.

And then new truths...

The truth is money is energy.
The truth is money is love.
The truth is I choose ease, grace, and flow in my relationship with money.
The truth is I love money and money loves me.
The truth I am worthy, valuable, lovable, successful, and safe, right here, right now, and always.
The truth is I am infinitely abundant.

The truth is my family and I are great with money.
The truth is I am a limitless gift to the world.
And so it is. And so much more.

Then Ben and I talked about how we were going to relate to this situation as a couple. We both took deep breaths and came up with a sound and grounded strategy for saving a bit each month to chip away at the tax bill.

"Should we cancel our trip to Austin to see your family?" Ben asked. "Is that too much right now?"

"No," I replied quickly. "I believe we just keep living the way we have been. That's how we can take our power back from money. Let's live the abundant, adventurous, and luscious life we've been living."

Ben agreed and that is just what we did. We chose to live free, even with the knowledge of the giant bill on the horizon. It wasn't always easy, and it was definitely an ever-unfolding navigation and learning. We explored a middle ground I can describe as "little to no attachment" with full engagement. In other words, we didn't totally dissociate from the tax bill completely. We saved money every month. At the same time, we didn't put our life on hold and *only* focus on the impending bill.

There is a quote by Rumi that says, "Out beyond the ideas of right-doing and wrongdoing there is a field. I will meet you there."

We lived in Rumi's field.

And then a miracle occurred.

As I was walking out of the local health food store, my cell phone rang. I looked down and it was my accountant again.

"Cora, I can't explain these numbers. I don't know what happened. But I ran your taxes for this year, and you don't owe *any* money. In fact, you actually receive money back. I'm shocked. There is really no logical explanation here."

I smiled, remembering, that this was also an opportunity not to give my power away to money. Sure, we had just found out the opposite news from before, but that didn't mean that I was any more free, abundant, or worthy than before.

So I took a deep breath and said, "Thank you so much Brian. I really appreciate this. You are a rockstar."

And I walked home to share the news with Ben. And of course Kirra.

We all could see the beauty and power in this unfolding. We noticed that money and energy flow in and out and all around, and it is always our *choice* in how to relate to this cycle. I could see that through this example and experience that I had taken my power back from money (to an extent) and learned how to *choose* to feel abundant, free, peaceful, trusting, secure no matter what the "money story" looked like moment to moment.

It was a monumental experience and one that I carry with me always. My life has never been the same. Between you and me, we eventually did end up paying that tax bill years later when it popped back up, and that was more than okay. By then, I had chosen to relate to money fully engaged, with little to no attachment, so I knew to just go with the flow and trust the process. I know now that all is well. Always.
This feels like true freedom. Financial freedom.

Do I still have debt? Yes.

Do I currently experience beautiful income? Yes.

Does any of this truly impact my true freedom? No.

And let me tell you, Little Coco, the one deep inside of me who filled the stockings with Happy Meal toys, *trusts* again.

What a limitless blessing.

And you thought financial freedom was about your financial situation!

Cora Poage is a Certified Holistic Health Coach through the Institute for Integrative Nutrition, and holds a Masters Degree in Spiritual Psychology from the University of Santa Monica.

Cora's specialty is in helping her clients align with their Soul and the Truth, fall in love with themselves, and align with their unique and Sacred Service on the planet. Cora believes that we when we align with our Soul and our Truth collectively, we create Heaven on Earth. To find out more about Cora please visit her at **corapoage.com.**

Growing Up Ritz

BY STEPH RITZ

While I have always been a Ritz, I've also spent most of my life hiding from my heritage—the name, notoriety, and enormity of living up to my potential. Can you imagine what it was like growing up the granddaughter of a famous self-made millionaire?

"The most you can do has to be done." My Grandma Ritz said these words during an acceptance speech when I was five. The phrase became my truth mantra.

Growing up Ritz, my normal included hanging out with presidents and dignitaries on school nights and watching my parents go out in fancy ball gowns and tuxedos a few times a week.

It was normal for me to get all dolled up, feeling on top of the world to be included in a big fancy gala, or get to go to the symphony, or some such schmoozy activity...and the very first moment you see Grandma Ritz she starts complaining about how you styled your hair and finds something wrong with the clothes you picked out for the evening.

I never considered Grandma Ritz's critiques as personal criticism; I understood she merely wanted me to be my best. Even as a kid, I understood Grandma Ritz's canary-yellow wool suit, while too itchy for snuggling, absolutely looked great on film in color AND in black and white newspaper photos.

The little girl in me didn't take it personally—instead I fell in love with the nuance of communicating both verbally and visually...

I understood my grandma needed to be a Ritz in those moments. She was doing so much more than merely being a grandma...she was changing the world.

My normal wasn't normal.

I think the first time I became consciously aware of my unusual family dynamic was the day I realized I had nowhere to go for "take your daughter to work day" because neither of my parents had jobs. We were living off of inheritance.

It was all any of us could do to hide how crazy my father was from the public eye. We lived in sheer terror inside my childhood home. The psychological evaluation during my parents' divorce revealed eleven diagnosable mental illnesses.

Outside of the public eye, abuse and neglect are the most basic words to describe what I experienced as a little girl. It took a long time to forgive my father. And it took even longer to forgive myself for believing it was normal to be abused and perpetuating the pattern throughout my life.

Behind the public eye, our millionaire grandmother was living a middle-class lifestyle...

When my brother asked for money from Grandma Ritz after his first year at a private college, she told us she had nothing left to give...It had all been put into irrevocable trusts donated as scholarships and trust funds to support leadership development for decades after her death.

Grandma Ritz had a vaulted room in her apartment (larger than my bedroom) filled with billions of dollars of artwork (also in trust funds), yet she lived on a fixed income. She was driving a dinged up Toyota and coupon-cutting over breakfast.

Grandma Ritz literally gave it all away.

She had expected my parents to create a college savings for us. They didn't. My parents lived a very lavish lifestyle. It was all a show, an act. Fueled by my dad's narcissism, a million dollars was spent all too quickly. Grandma Ritz expected too much of my mentally ill father, and it was too late for her to do anything about it.

I saw firsthand what it really meant to create a lasting legacy beyond one's own lifetime—to understand how wealth can directly correlate to bettering billions of people's futures.

How amazing to see my philanthropist grandmother's fortune help so many others, to see the oil paintings I'd run my fingers over countless times (*shhh,* don't tell) now hanging in museums around the world.

And I also learned to value the things money can't buy, like appreciating the time you have with someone, not knowing how long (or brief) it will last...

When my mom and step-dad died two years apart from each other, I inherited a beautiful collection of paintings, prints, rights-of-reproductions, and sketches from a world-famous artist. Yet there wasn't much money in the bank. And I was definitely about to accrue some hefty bills as I separated a hoarder's stash of treasures from the creative endeavors of my step-dad, Stanley Meltzoff.

It didn't surprise me when my first year of sales as an entrepreneur grossed just shy of half a million. I simply did what needed to be done.

You see, when a famous artist dies, their art becomes much more valuable...or the artist slides into obscurity. It was in every collector's interest to boost the credibility of canvases they'd invested in years before.

Some of the largest collectors of my step-dad's artwork were publishers, really well-known millionaire business tycoons. These men didn't only want more Stanley Meltzoff art; they wanted to get their hands on his unpublished autobiography.

There's no amount of money that could have aligned everything so perfectly.

My mom had prepped me more than I knew. In the months leading up to her death, we'd talk once a week and she'd tell me how my step-dad's dying wish was to publish his autobiography. My mom told me how unhappy she was with the direction one publisher was trying to take the book project—how Stanley would be mortified to see the integrity of the book demolished.

I never found a contract with a publisher. Nothing besides the memory of my mom telling me about the situation.

I also remembered loving the books published by one of the largest collectors of my step-dad's canvases, Mike Rivkin.

So I invited Rivkin to come for a private viewing, and I set up the first floor of the house to be a gallery.

Some of the art had never been seen before, having been cataloged and photographed just months before as part of my training with my mom. On the good days, she's sit bundled up in her fuzzy pink blanket on the couch in the studio, pointing and directing me through the process of documenting hundreds of sketches from World War II. My step-dad was an award-winning political cartoonist for the Army newspaper, which is still in print today. Sketches of all sizes in various mediums were soon going to be available to the public. They were exquisite!

Mike Rivkin was the first to access these never-before-seen sketches and never-available-to-the-public oil paintings. It was the perfect deal-sweetener to entice him to publish my step-dad's autobiography. It was my parents' dying wish to get it published...

And wouldn't you know it? He had brought his checkbook.

With $90,000 paid in full up front, Rivkin and I began a year's dive into leaving a lasting legacy for my step-dad. I focused on generating buyer leads and creating an integrated online marketing system to sell all the artwork on our website—and made sure to position the art I'd inherited into the pages of the book.

It was easy to sell the entire business once it was all separated from the house, fully cataloged, photographed, published in a book, with a proven online sales system.

I remember the exact moment when the universe decided for me...

I found myself in a nearly identical position to one of my favorite canvases in my newly inherited collection—"Unfinished Bridge"—a self-portrait of my step-dad at twenty-five sitting on the edge of the Brooklyn Bridge before it was built, trying to decide what to do with his life. A year later, World War II broke out, and the military decided for him...

There I was at the ripe ol' age of twenty-six, a year into entrepreneurship with a lucrative business now perfectly positioned into a gorgeous coffee table book, and my marketing had proven to cold-convert into sales.

I was in New York City, an hour's drive from where I was living in Stanley's house in New Jersey, stomping pavement down in the Financial District, lost in thought after negotiations for wall space at the Society of Illustrators on the Upper West Side for my step-dad's book launch.

In that moment I realized I had just spent a year of my life giving every ounce of energy to a business I was not being paid to run!

Done. Gone. Time to get out.

My second contract with the publisher was selling him the perfectly positioned and neatly organized business. I let Rivkin make an offer before approaching any other potential buyers (you better believe I made sure he knew he was getting special treatment) and I accepted the first offer. I was confident the buyer's value far surpassed the product cost. Less than half a million was cheap! A steal! Liquidated rates...

And can I tell you how grateful I was to be selling the whole thing to the publisher, co-author, and heavily invested collector?

Yet the perception of earning six figures is not what it seems...

With a hefty chunk coming off the top for taxes, and huge amount spent sorting the business from the house and preserving the art, that only left around one-third as income. And I only owned one-third of the business.

So I returned to Wisconsin, finished the last semester of my undergraduate degree, and took on more writing projects, creating books, articles, and copywriting for websites.

One of the first articles I co-wrote (under a pen name in the cannabis industry) was published as the centerfold in High Times Magazine, an eleven-page spread in their 420th special edition. I've been told it's their longest article published, and that 500,000 copies were distributed around the world. I still find it mind-bending...Insta-fame. Again. Fame was my normal from growing up Ritz, and now I had become famous under a different name because of truly wanting to make a difference.

I was doing the most I could do to change the integrity of an industry with the potential to change millions of lives.

But my career flipped upside down when a combination of illnesses knocked out my immune system—a parting "gift" from the hospital while terminal caregiving for a relative I'd looked after for eleven years.

The longer I was in bed, the less I asked for my work...I was in-and-out of the hospital, often bedridden, never knowing when the next wave of sickness would knock me down to the ground again. If I couldn't trust my body, how could I ask someone else to trust me?

I went from five-figure contracts down to an hourly rate of $50.

And while stuck in bed, I taught myself how to build a Wordpress website one frosty winter weekend back in Wisconsin when I decided to build an online business for myself.

It was truly beautiful to see my website come to life over a few long days...I created a series of pages and opt-ins that were cold-converting, with services, sales pages, verbal and visual branding, menus, widgets, and a mailing list. As it turns out, the system I set up back in 2013 was extremely comprehensive and cutting edge.

Taking on the challenge of building a website and sales page system for myself was totally my idea of a *fun* weekend activity. I never questioned if I could; I simply did what needed to be done. And I needed a website.

Now that I'd built a stellar website, how was I going to show potential clients I was the right person to pull the right stories out of them? How could I provide value far beyond expectations? I'd been writing under a pseudonym, so I couldn't share my prior projects. Ah, yes...I'd start a video interview series!

The second person I interviewed converted into a client.

After our work together, my client, Meilin, went from speaking to a few hundred people at trade shows every couple of months near her home in Germany to a bi-weekly audience of over 200,000 on her own online radio show where she channels shamanic sound healings. Meilin saw my true expertise...

Writing with a shaman was like nothing I'd ever experienced.

Often, we'd get on the phone, talk for a few minutes, review where we'd been and where we were going, and eventually we'd both lapse into silence. That's when things started to get strange. Her words would flow from my fingertips while we worked in near silence. I was merely an open channel giving shape and form to her heart message—pages upon pages created though unspoken communication.

Being interconnected in thought scared me.

I didn't tell anyone how this German shaman and I had worked together. I started doubting the whole experience, even though we wrote like this a dozen times over many months working together.

It wasn't until years later when I finally accepted I had a gift...

I told another shaman, Rafael, that he was in my dreams that night, having met the day before at a business conference. I dreamt we sat on the ground, knee to knee, facing one another at the top of a mountain in Mexico. That we were having the most in-depth conversation while sitting in silence, never a word spoken out loud. How we were talking about how to raise money to educate children in areas where basic needs aren't being met— how to address the struggle of balancing surviving with teaching the tools to move beyond survival.

Rafael said he'd had the same dream! What a *whoa* moment!

A few months later, Rafael and I sat knee to knee for real. With a hand on each of my kneecaps, he poured energy into my body, willing me to accept that I was a healer too.

And I knew what I had to do: It was time to embrace the millionaire's mindset I'd inherited.

A few days after this profound life-altering eye-opening soul-purpose was revealed to me, I asked to share my story from the stage at an upcoming business event for entrepreneurs put on by two of my business coaches. They said yes, and I created a ten-minute signature stage talk to vulnerably share my truth.

From the stage, I shared about fulfilling my parents' dying wishes, writing for millionaires and billionaires, losing my immune system and being bedridden, having my ex-boyfriend break one of my ribs, moving across the country to heal in the giant redwoods, and how I'd systematized my unique process into group retreats and online courses so my ideas could be accessible to people who aren't earning seven+ figures yet.

What I've learned is that when you feel you're between a rock and a hard place...it is a door opening into a new future. You don't have to be ready when opportunity knocks, you just have to say *yes*.

While I might not have earned a billion dollars (yet), I am humbled and awed knowing I've impacted millions of lives by trusting what I know to be true.

At every turn, I've trusted the ground beneath my feet. I have moved forward with a deep knowing that where I thought I should be might not actually be the best place for me. My place, here and now, has been curated by my choices—and it can always change.

I appreciate Grandma Ritz's millionaire mindset training more each day, especially how it led me to my own truth mantra:

~What you are is greater than anything you have experienced.
~Who you are is bigger than you currently dare to imagine.
~Your dreams are only a reflection of who you realistically can become.
~Start imagining what you—as a limitless human being—truly have the power to accomplish.

So please ask yourself: What is the most you can do? Because that is what has to be done.

BREATH IN. BREATHE OUT.

Money in.
Money out.

Money in:
Accept what is,
Manifest what could be...

Money out:
Accept what isn't,
Let go of what was...

Money in:
Accept the journey,
Share in abundance...

Money out:
Make room for what will come,
Clear space to receive...

Money in.
Money out.

Go with the flow.

Breathe in.
Breathe out.

Steph Ritz is known for turning what you're saying into what you meant to say. As a visual and verbal communication expert, Steph guides you to develop a visionary brand presence. For over fourteen years, she's guided internationally acclaimed artists, marketers, healers, educators, coaches, and corporations to use crystal clear communication and cutting edge marketing strategies.

When Steph's parents passed away two years apart, suddenly Steph was the only person left living that knew the stories behind world-famous paintings. She put her life on hold for a year and published her step-dad's autobiography. Together with the publisher, Steph redesigned the book project and it's now a stunning art book fully integrated with an online marketing system that, ten years later, still stands strong. After fulfilling her parents' dying wish, Steph continued with a career as a writing coach, website designer, photographer, and speaker.

She's helped clients grow their radio audience into hundreds of thousands, get movie contracts with the potential to reach a billion homes, and write sales page systems that make millions of dollars. Steph has a reputation as a master word weaver—rebranding entire industries, entrepreneurs, and business owners. She guides you to voice your passions with words that change the world.

Steph Ritz is obsessed with writing that converts, and if you're an entrepreneur you ought be too. Invite your tribe to experience the same things you saw in your journey to becoming the expert you are today. Why use stories in your copywriting? Storytelling is a remarkable way to set yourself up to succeed with proper positioning stories for you, your products, and your brand.

Special Gift

Visit **stephritz.com/bonus** to get instant access to "Epic Story Prompts For Entrepreneurs: How To Position Yourself As An Expert In Your Writing"—Steph Ritz's world-renowned quick start guide to make copywriting easy!

ABUNDANCE I

Awaken my Heart
to the Light of possibility.
Flood my soul
with the magnitude of gratitude.

Quelch my energetic field
with rainbow vibrations.
Seed my thirsting garden
with showers of inspiration.

Hail roots of life's garden,
intertwine with mine,
as continuum I
embrace the DIVINE.

ABUNDANCE II

The Inbreath of All
melds
acceptance and transmutation
into
the Outbreath of LOVE.

ABUNDANCE III

Falling in the sacred space,
of Heart's deepening.
Listening,
into the expanse of seeming silence.
No words cutting,
dividing,
nor portioning
the Eternal into bite-size.

Ethers conversing,
overtones dancing,
in–spir–ation,
angelically descending,
unwrapping–unfolding
Liminal, boundless desire.

American-born **Eàsula Sedlmaier** has spent most of her bi-lingual life in Germany. More than thirty years of international coaching and training experience have allowed her to meld her educational background in psychology, philosophy, art, dance, meditation, and Intentional Creativity into a powerful mix which she utilizes for offerings in transformational coaching and retreats for women. Along with her creative skills as author, painter and shamanic circle rites holder she facilitates women in reconnecting to their inner wisdom and Divine feminine energy.

Her work with individuals as well as groups presently has a shamanic nature and allows her to create sacred space and open up into sacred portals of deeper knowledge and experience. She describes her work as a journey through portals and gateways.

With the completion of her qualification in 2016 as an Intentional Creativity Teacher she now officially holds creative heart space and journeys with others, so that they can access their own stories and information and bring that into a sacred art form and fuller expression. Eàsula has found that creativity can be a very effective gateway to some of our deepest emotions and encoded knowledge.

In-between preparing her healing art for various local exhibitions in Germany, she creates and guides others in a dialogue with the inner sacred feminine. Her practice involves deep listening to the magic that happens first in the void; to then appear during the journeying, visioning and tarot usage. She has been quoted as saying: "What inflames my passion? Peeling back layers of illusions and experience so that the radiance of Essence can shine through. Learn more at **roaring-hearts.com.**

Re-Story-ing Our Economy: Living the Path to Prosperity

BY SAMANTHA SWEETWATER

"There is no away."

~JULIA BUTTERFLY HILL

I am a human, and as a human, I, like you, I am a story making machine. As a co-creator with the universe and with all of life, I live the stories I tell about what I expect my life to be like, who and what I think I am or can be, what is possible, how the world works, what is meaningful, valuable or worthy, and what my life, love, time, labor, and wisdom are worth. Story drives motive, which drives desire, which drives action.

Change the story, change everything.

Economy is a big story. The word *economy* is borrowed from the Latin *oeconomia*, meaning "management of the household," derived from *oîkos*, "house" and *némō*, "distribute or allocate." Our current global economy is a collective story and set of behaviors defining how we keep our house— that is, our planet, our culture, and our relationship. This is the macro-economy. Economy is also personal and individual; it's your participation in and co-creation of a vast meshwork of sovereign entities attached to unique stories, motives, and actions. This is microeconomics. You and I collectively contribute to this, thus systemically co-steering the direction of our world.

This particular economy is grounded in a set of assumptions about possession, ownership, commodification, and how uneven distribution and embedded scarcity co-generate wealth. It is founded in dominion over and separation from nature and the soul.

In the current story, insecurity is the foundation of a scarcity-based system in which individuals use economics in an effort to increase personal security.

In the current economy, the elephant in the room, the belief that underlies all other beliefs, is the story of scarcity. But you have a game-changing power. You get to chose whether or not you believe in, enact, and transact that story.

The stories you tell and live are power.

Our current economy is just a sucky set of stories for explaining the value of what a human being, in all of her creative glory and capacity, really is. Our current economy is lousy at integrating the nuanced magic of the soul, or at valuing natural living systems, or at accounting for the externalized impacts our current system takes for granted.

While many of us in the consciousness community have done fantastic work to reframe our relationships with money, our infinite nature, and the value of our creativity and energy, that doesn't account for the philosophical and material biases embedded in our current macro-economic practices of profit and money that are systemically pathological to our survival and thrival as a species. An economy that makes invisible the use and abuse of nature is not one that will get us to prosperity. And, honestly, it pisses me off when spiritual people say "money is just energy," and "you are infinite," because it veils the reality that our current monetary system is based on a value standard that is harmful to life itself. Money is symbolic energy that is moored to a vast network of complex relationships and to value standards. When we pretend that money (in its current form) is neutral, we obscure the creative and ethical traction that we *do* have when we engage the economy and which is non-optional to creating a system that is truly prosperous. We gloss what needs to change about the value standards underneath our currencies if we want to cause long-term thriving.

Don't get me wrong. I'm not against money. I'm *for* evolving it. I'm in the game of using our current monetary system to bootstrap the next level of our evolution. This begins on the outer level by creating win-win exchanges, stewarding soul-centric value, and crafting regenerative models for business and design. It begins on the inner level with deconstructing scarcity, embodying abundance, embodying generosity, and creating (monetary) value around what we feel really matters, such as experience, beauty, the sacred, earth stewardship and things that cause happiness and real health. If you're in the business of creating from your soul and your true purpose, if you're stewarding what you love, creating monetary worth around what you do is an important part of turning the macro-tides.

My endgame is an economy and diversified monetary system conducive to the thriving of our local ecosystems, the biosphere as a whole, people, and diverse cultures. We can do it. And we have to. We're in a rocky transition phase. It's going to get weirder and more turbulent before it gets stable. And it is my strong belief and vision that the best way to cause prosperity for one's self and one's family is to approach one's engagement with the current economy as a means to steward the new economy.

It's time for win-win economics.

I love the title of this book: *Pioneering the Path to Prosperity*. I ask, what does that mean? Distinct from debates about the better, or least bad system—Capitalism, Socialism, Marxism, any *-ism*—what *is* prosperity? The very title suggests that the path we're currently on isn't prosperous. So, what does pioneering a new path look like? What edges are we pushing? What values are we embodying? How does prosperity look, feel, and act? If "there's no away," how do we integrate that into how we engage wealth?

Personal prosperity isn't a set metric. It's not a function of the gross domestic product. It isn't a place you arrive. It's a process. It's both an inner game—a mental, emotional, and spiritual state of being—and an outer game that we're playing in a world that has an extremely strong set of stories about what constitutes success, where value comes from, how economy works, and what it is supposed to enable over time.

Prosperity isn't the same thing as abundance. While abundance is something that happens in the present moment, prosperity is something intergenerational that happens over time. Our current economy tells a story about economic progress that is unconcerned with who wins, who loses, or what is lost in the path of progress. It tells a story about value that is grounded in scarcity while telling a story about progress and profit based on a (false) assumption of limitless physical resources. Mythologically, it is both the child of resource extraction and endless expansion. It is interested solely in gain. It lacks coherent narratives of reciprocity, regenesis, contribution, collaboration, shareability, or response-ability. It gets limitlessness wrong because it fails to account for limits.

Our current economy tells a story about economic progress that is unconcerned with who wins, who loses, or what is lost in the path of progress.

If you are a winner in this system, you have to grapple with the reality that your win implies many losers. Success, in the current system, comes, by definition, at the expense of other people and ecosystems.

While being financially successful is one meaningful aspect of prosperity, I implore you to look deeper. What if the current finance system isn't one that can cause long-term systemic success? What if personal success, as currently defined, comes at the expense of the future of all, and therefore also the future of the individual? To be prosperous is to cause abundance for one's self, for one's family, and for the world over the arc of time. If you or I are going to pioneer a path to real prosperity, we're going to need to change some things.

The bummer is this: Our current economic story completely obscures the direct relationship between human economic activities and our environment, because it considers environmental factors to be "externalities" which are not considered in the cost of goods or services. In other words, the current economy (and how we measure profit in it) externalizes everything necessary for future prosperity and survival to the human species. Profit, as currently practiced, is pathological.

The current economy externalizes the impacts and costs we must integrate in order to cause a thriving and prosperous future for ourselves and our descendants. Profit, as currently practiced, is pathological.

Our current economy is founded in Genesis' concept of dominion over nature. On this basis, ownership and commodification were made possible (and labeled "natural") and profit (as currently defined) was created. On this basis, an economy separate from the earth and the soul was created. It grew to enslave living human beings while building a thriving international trade in sugar, cotton, tobacco, and alcohol. Then, industrialization happened, birthing economies of scale. A global war engine was built. And onwards we grew, birthing trans-global tech, the Information Age, and now the Age of Experience.

We've been so successful in our expansion that geologists now call this time on the planet the Anthroposcene—the geological epoch within which human and technological endeavor has become the most prominent force of evolution on our planet, so much so that it can be measured in geological terms.

The path we're on, both in macro and most microeconomic dimensions, is a win-lose game where winning is at the expense of some*one* or some-*where* else. Success is defined as being on the positive side of a zero-sum game. If you are reading this, regardless of how successful you *feel*, you are probably a winner in the game, which means someone else lost for you to get here. Is this really winning?

If there is such a thing as profit in the future, it will be inseparable from regenerative metrics. Profit that isn't regenerative is ultimately existential and, therefore, not long-term profitable.

True profit is life-positive.

Serious talk.

I don't need you to agree with me. I'm being provocative.

I want to give you some things to chew on, to encourage the brilliant new thoughts, ideas, business models, or community initiative you might come up with. I trust you...Or, more accurately, I trust us. I trust us in the sense that I trust the soul. I trust that the soul of each individual and the oversoul of humanity has, within the sacred ecology of the great symphony of our creativity, all the next steps and solutions we could ever need to thrive. And, I trust the way life's impulse lives and breathes so indomitably through our creativity and our love, always seeking to enable more life. Try this trust on. It feels good.

Now I'd like put all the pieces together by sharing a vision that was given to me. It's a vulnerable sharing, but I can't send this chapter to print without it. So...here it is, a vision that fundamentally recalibrated my understanding of what is possible through love-aligned economics.

One vision can change everything.

Here's the scene: I'm lying with my eyes closed in the dark. The music pulses through me. I feel embraced in an almost intolerable beauty and more alive than life itself.

I've come to the other side of the planet to sit with Ayahuasca, the sacred vine, Queen of the Forest, whose healing and capacity for transmission has become globally legendary in recent years. She has a great deal to say to me on this night. Her terms and metaphors are completely palpable and clear.

All night long, this masterful teacher plant, *Madre Ayahuasca*, pumps me with a golden flow of true abundance. She shows me the sacred math my soul instinctively understands. She says, shape your concept of money *like* life, and you will manifest true abundance and wealth. She says, life wants money to work the way life works—as a meta-force mediating the ongoing evolution of complexity, diversity, and harmony in living systems. Since those living systems are now profoundly shaped by human co-creation, it is up to you humans to create an economy that accounts for your true interdependence with all of life. It's sacred math, and it's the only true path to your prosperity. Money will just be better, and more valuable, if it works *with* life rather than against it.

She explains to me that money, when it is in integrity with life, is indeed a flow of pure energy, and that the energy is the pure gold of life-force itself, also related to water (a mystery I don't yet fully understand). To be more abundant, I must expand the aperture of the flow of life through me. (She's cheering me on.) Just having money flow, without life, is a death force, devoid of color or any true intelligence (from her perspective). As the aperture of the life force expands and is connected to money, that is true prosperity.

She shows me, in thousands of ways, the deeper logic of economy on life's terms. She shows me that there is really no such thing as prosperity separate from reciprocity, and that to be abundant is to increase giving and receiving. Life builds on connections, makes waste into resource, and networks diversity to create greater intelligence and resilience. Life trades up to make more of itself. Life knows nothing as separate. To be abundant is to collaborate with and co-design with life, in the deepest terms, and so expand the rainbow of the soul's manifestation of God's mind.

She shows me—a message I've received many times before in other ways—that the design of soul is the holographic double of life's ecology. Soul ecology and life's ecology are one and the same thing. And, that to create our world as a reflection of life and as a liberation of soul is *the pathway to true prosperity.*

She shows me that currencies—not just money as we currently conceive it, but any exchange of energy that can be seen, named, and honored as valuable—that flow in the direction of greater harmony, reciprocity, respect, learning, natural growth, creativity, soul-integrity, beauty, and networked intelligence follow the true path of gold. They are the frequency of gold, the very same thing as the mineral we have given such value to, only in multi-dimensional form.

She makes it clear that I, as a sovereign and infinitely creative being, regardless of the form of the economy I'm living within, can channel money, resources, energy, time, and ultimately love through my limitless vision and capacity to increase the flows of life that move through me, my relationships, my businesses, and my message. Both the limits and the limitless matter. Wisdom is embodying and loving them both.

She says, "Be golden. Share more. Let more flow through you."

Be golden.

Share more.

Let more flow through you.

In my altered state, my witness consciousness is still strong. I think to myself, *All my life, I've been seeking to live what she is showing me, yet I've been timid, unsure. Now, it is clear to me. Now I know what true prosperity feels like, how it behaves, what frequency it operates at, how it is limitless in energy and information, yet grounded and shaped by the wise limits of living systems, and that it flows where life and love grow. Yup. I'm all in.*

"Now," She says, "make it real."

I am a channel of the new economy.

It took me about three years to integrate that vision. For the first two, I was busy living through the initiatory bumps and bruises of a solopreneur in major life and business transition. I moved twice and flirted with a career as a Hollywood producer (I love to tell stories). Then, about a year ago, I received an immensely clear message to follow my prayers back to the Bay Area to serve my higher purpose.

A significant part of my higher purpose, as my plant guide affirmed, is to co-create a new economy that is soul-centric, life-positive, and conducive to the thriving evolution of life on this planet. From a purely analytical perspective, this seems both inevitable yet awkwardly improbable. Here's why: I have no business school or economics background. I grew up in a family where my parents worked regular jobs. Neither one of them have an entrepreneurial bone in their body. I received *zero* hours of financial education growing up—either at home or in school. And, while I've done decently well for myself as a serial entrepreneur and transformational facilitator, I never considered myself to be particularly good at doing business or at making money. So, getting the call to influence the future of the macro-economy felt pretty audacious and wonky.

But, hey, the combined ingredients of audacity, hard work, and sacred vision are pretty strong stuff. Indeed, that's pretty much all that has ever created worlds.

So, here we are, my friend.

We are here to re-store-y this global economy together. There is not one way. There are many ways and many iterations. It's going to take all the codes each of us carry. We may not each see it in the same way, but if we bring our love, creativity, collaboration, and true commitment to the well-being of the whole to the game, I think *we* can win.

Let's do it. Take my hand.

I no longer accept scarcity in my space.
I declare that my Space is the planet.

~ All Love ~

Samantha Sweetwater is an urban shaman, Integrated Brilliance Coach, serial soulpreneur, and author. She is loved internationally as a guide whose no-BS healing and coaching empower evolutionary leaders to get out of the way, manifest inspiration, and exponentiate impact through fully embodied purpose.

As a spiritual leader, wisdom teacher, and systems theorist with more than 25 years of facilitation experience and a vast background in embodiment (somatics, choreography, dance, raja yoga, chi kung, meditation, transpersonal psychology, and permaculture), a bachelor's degree in Legal Philosophy and Dance, and a master's degree in Integral Wisdom Studies, she architects experiences that support core level healing and alignment of soul, nature, and source. She embodies a tender, rigorous, and fierce love and invites you to lead and love as what you know to be True.

As a serial soulpreneur she has pushed the edge of culturally recognized value and helped to create the industry of Conscious Dance. Samantha is the former founder of Dancing Freedom (2000) the Peacebody School Japan (2006), through which she built and scaled a global movement of embodied awakening that touched tens of thousands of lives on five continents, trained hundreds of facilitators, and co-created tens of localized hubs for transformational community. She is the current founder and spiritual director of One Life Circle, providing an intimate community of practice and prayer in the San Francisco Bay Area dedicated to evolving love, leadership, and purpose in service to the One Life we all share. She is a featured author in *The New Feminine Evolutionary* published by Flower of Life Press. Her next book, *Everyone Comes Home*, will release in 2019. Learn more at **SamanthaSweetwater.com.**

The Phoenix Effect:
From the Fire Springs New Life

BY SCOTT WATROUS

Writing about money, prosperity, and abundance seems like it should be an easy task, right? Just share your story. Well, I've come to find out that I have absolutely no relationship with money at all. Sounds kind of hard to believe for someone of a certain age, who has gone through quite a bit of money in my time. How could I have no relationship with it? How can I have bought million-dollar homes, nice cars, and luxury vacations without having a relationship with money? As I write this chapter and review my story I realize that money and I weren't friends or enemies...we just didn't really know each other.

As a kid, my parents provided everything that I could have ever wanted. Not luxury, but good solid things and the freedom to do whatever we desired. I'm sure my parents felt financial pressure, but my dad kept it to himself, and my mother was always moving too fast on some project or plan to worry much about anything.

My first real job working for the publisher Simon and Schuster didn't pay too much, but I got a car and expense account, and I was free to live the life I wanted to on the roads and byways of New England. Every year from when I got that first serious job until I left the corporate world thirty years later, I made more money every year. It was a fast track career, and I left my finances in the hands of whoever my partner was at the time. The money flowed, and we spent it as fast as possible!

EGO

Ego and money are tied tightly for most of us, and my self-image was polished by my nonchalant attitude about it. I wasn't ostentatious in an obnoxious way (at least I don't think so!), but all of the signs were there: my wrist sported a Rolex, my garage filled with two fast cars just for me, and an air of superiority reigned that pains me to recall. My drive wasn't fueled by the dream of more luxury, yet money was the currency of my interface with the world, and my decisions assumed that I would always be in the flow of wealth.

WASTEFUL HABITS

I moved ten times in fifteen years, each new place bigger than the last until I stepped away from my comfortable world of salaries and bonuses. Each house required new stuff, more stuff, and of course a dumpster to fill with the detritus of silly purchases and wasted ideas.

I never stopped to think, *what does this say about me?* Everything was replaceable, and I didn't have the respect for what *stuff* really meant.

Lawnmowers are the perfect example of my detachment: the money that bought them held little meaning for me, therefore my mowers ran until they didn't anymore—no oil changes required—and storage outside during winter? Suggested only! Any problems? Take the old one to the dump, buy a new one, and voilà! Not just cheap push-mowers either—a couple of fancy riders found the dump, too!

As I look back on that time in my life, I was awash in abundance. My jobs were dream gigs for me. I did it "my way" with a belief system built on intellectual superiority and utter confidence. I never doubted myself, and though it sounds awfully vain now, I exuded power—and when I turned it on, look out!

I was a master of "the game," that one-upmanship that permeates corporations, organizations, and almost any group of people thrown together. The trick to "the game" was to undermine others—and not get caught. The dishonesty seemed benign at the time, because when I believed I was *right...* it was too easy to roll over people and never look back.

At Random House in the 90's, the joke was "Be careful when you leave your office...someone else might be at your desk when you get back!" It was like that TV show *Survival*, everyone vying to stay one step ahead, hoping their subterfuge didn't get uncovered around the fire. I entered that world as a naive country boy from rural Pennsylvania—and emerged fourteen years later with all cylinders firing on high-octane fuel, ready for a decade filled with power, money, and an absolute belief in myself.

Abundance surrounded me, and I don't mean just the financial windfalls and objects acquired. My ex-wife and I had conceived a beautiful boy, and he had a farm to roam on, with dogs, cats, three goats and a rabbit to keep him company. This was the American Dream, white picket fence and everything! I was President of a publishing company with 225 employees, I made lots of money, and when I come home, my blond-cherub son Alden would run into my arms, followed by a phalanx of critters. It sounds like everyone's dream come true, right?

But it wasn't my dream. I never really had a *desire* about my life's path, and through my power I kept creating new opportunities. That's the crazy part—I was a master "manifester" who always saw the goal, and never doubted my ability to make it happen. I was considerate of my employees, at least the ones who were *part of the solution*...I disregarded the rest as part of the problem.

My life was fabulous! Travel anytime, anywhere. Eat at the most fabulous places! Buy cars with cash. And here is the other part that made it so easy to disregard money and it's meaning: expenses accounts. From my first job at Simon & Schuster, I used my Amex card without regard, and as an executive at Random House, the money flowed, along with company cars and perks.

So when the stock market crashed in 2008, and the divorce proceedings burned up stacks of green, well, bottom line: the money started to run out, and I felt helpless. I had never really worked alone, and my team of kick-ass employees were no more. Something had to crack, and it was me.

DOWN

The dark side showed itself subtly, fractures missed while in the thrall of my own ego-driven fast track to destruction. It's a long story, and as time passes, the details mean less and less. It hurts, deeply, to relive the destruction of divorce and separation from my kids—the rest of it is just words, like *stock market crash, mortgage default,* or *bankruptcy.* I lost money like I spent it, with no connection to what it meant to my happiness, and no fear of what it might be like to be broke.

My heart was broken, a zillion pieces of love falling like confetti into a muck of pain, guilt, and shame like a dark cave that barely held any light.

REBIRTH

It's a strange time to be a man. The defining elements of masculinity are in flux like never before—almost every moment, the old ideals and definitions of **men** are stripped of their stories and shredded like yellowed paper— leaving an empty space where the ground used to be.

We are a product of all that came before: *millions of years hunting, farming, and letting nature show us who we needed to be if we wanted to survive.* Our DNA holds tightly to the millennia of experience—*men as dominant forces, evolving within a world confined by geography and lacking in the modalities of communication we take for granted.* Without any context other than survival, men *evolved* to meet the needs of the ecosystem they inhabited...and it worked very, very well—until technology erased millions of years of adaptation in this crazy cycle of constant change.

So where does *prosperity* fit into this swirl of confusion? What drives men forward, lights the spark, fuels the *new evolution?* What are we going to choose for ourselves and our struggling world?

My comfortable life in the matrix of corporations left me disconnected from *heart.* I was missing the deeper love that goes beyond sex and romance and the inevitable and assumed breakup from difficult relationships. My story of rebirth begins in the woods...nine acres of riverside hills and trails, flora and fauna spread across Gaia's tapestry with the master's brush. Each day I walked the paths etched by the People—native spirits holding space in the ethereal—deer, fox and coyote following the contours of the land, guiding my journey.

Every day I set out on an adventure into my forest. One path led to the river—eagles and ospreys watching my progress with cries of joyous freedom. Another cut along the hillside above the marsh, a myriad of water, woods, and birds telling their stories—one message, one voice, and infinite language.

I cut wood.

Our earth gave me the gift of cedar trees—skeletons standing tall—leafless, yet alive with scent and color, victims of some blight or deep freeze of long ago.

Nature's incredible abundance gave me hope, filling me with a joy that I had long ago forgotten. But I still knew nothing about how to handle money in my life.

BANKRUPTCY

Damn, that's a loaded word. *Bankrupt: Any insolvent debtor; a person unable to satisfy any just claims made upon him or her.*

Bankruptcy changes *everything!* No cushion, no last resort/worry about it when the bill comes. Money comes directly from *intention, action,* and a *resonance of self-love and openness to receiving the bounty* that the Universe holds for each of us.

The judgment of the social and financial matrix is long out of my grid, so I don't feel shame or guilt about that, except as it affects my kids and my difficulty in paying child support. When the end of the month draws near, I panic and draw inward, which just perpetuates the problem. *Inward* can be a place of enlightenment, or a trap of inaction—a center of transformation when Spirit shines light, or a place to hide from the 3D reality. Oh, it's a shitty feeling, and the only freedom is to change, *evolve!* Sadness, helplessness, and defeat breeds more of the same, until the stink of my own dirty bath water finally coalesces into a *choice:* shift the vibration, clear the trash can, and *evolve*—or go pull the pillow over my head and suffer.

THE POWER TO CHANGE

I am blessed with *knowing* how to shift, and grateful for the gift of understanding the dynamics of change. I use my tools: mindfulness, empathy, and the biggest one of all—love. "All you need is love" sounds so simple, yet, when you apply a bit of science and Quantum Awareness to the challenge there is a timeless Universal Law that can offer tangible results, instantly!

The Law of the Perpetual Transmutation of Energy sounds complicated, yet it encompasses the power of your subtle body to make change happen in your life, and hold a resonance of love and freedom. *Transmuting* is basically creating a vibration *opposite of your obstacle,* and focusing on *feeling* that positive vibration without thinking about the problem.

Here is what you need to know in order to use this to clear your path to prosperity:

ENERGY: understanding, visualizing, and managing your energetic profile is the key to reprogramming any negativity or blockages around *anything in your Quantum Grid.*

- Negative thoughts create low-vibration in your Subtle Body
- Those vibrations are *resonating points* in the Quantum Grid
- The chakras and meridians of your energy system *transmit your emotions* and set the vibration of your connection to the Universal Grid
- The Universal Law of Cause and Effect dictates that your *transmission* will be received by the Universe, and will transmit the same vibration back to you

What's your story? If you feel in a state of "lack," talk about your money problems with others, and fear the life that is unfolding before you, your grid will only attract more of the situations and negative experiences that you want to avoid, and your story will become your life. Take charge and create something different!

MY PRACTICE

If you meditate or practice mindfulness, you already know the power of silence, and the clear thoughts and truths that can flower from quieting your subconscious. My journey would never have started without meditation. The space of truth isn't in this 3D bandwidth that we call home, nor is it within the constant drone of voices that sow doubt and judgment. The "work" of conscious evolution happens within the chalice of *Spirit,* that flow of light, information, and pure love residing within your heart and soul.

Be mindful. Find the voice of your highest power. Listen. Set your intention. *Evolve...*

My daily practice always includes several deep meditations, either with Sacred music (OM chants and Tibetan bowls are great), silence, or by being outside, embraced by Gaia's symphony.

In the meditative space, I acknowledge the issue that I am struggling with, then focus completely on something else—in my case, my kids. I see them, feel their hugs, smell their hair, love them without edges...The trick is to let the love flow unimpeded, no words or thinking, just the pure river of love—the **vibration** of an open heart, smiling faces, and the *freedom to love...*

When you practice this regularly, you will truly be amazed at how quickly your "problem" disappears from your grid. It's alchemy and particle manipulation catalysts by the wonderful vibration of *love...*

LAST WORDS

Today, I am so grateful to be alive and open to the possibility of abundance in every moment. My bank account still hasn't filled up, but I know it will. I will honor the greenbacks when they arrive, since money is just one way of receiving the abundance of Spirit, one fractal in a myriad of gifts that await all beings who have the courage to evolve past their story of lack and woe. *I desire prosperity in my life.* It takes work, struggle, and the courage to change. I have the power to make it happen. It is my decision. And yours. The journey continues.

Scott Watrous brings thirty-five years of publishing and branding experience to his work as an Evolutionary Coach, Cannabis consultant/advocate, marketing strategist and kick-ass copywriter. He has two children, three stepdaughters, and lives on the Connecticut coast with his wife Jane Ashley.

Special Gift

Visit **fireheartcoaching.com** to get your free copy of
"The Fireheart Guide to the Universal Laws".

ACKNOWLEDGMENTS

Thank you to the authors for your willingness to be in service and vulnerably share your stories:

Alexis Neely
Tanya Lynn Paluso
Alis Mao
Alokananda
Olana Barros
Rima Bonario
Allison Conte
Lainie Love Dalby
Dana Damara
Aurora Farber
Nicole Hemmer
Cristina Laskar
Grace Lawrence
Amanda Leigh
Megan Luther
Mia Luz
Maribeth Morrissey
Kate Mulder
Alexandra Pallas
Gavin Pauley
Cora Poage
Steph Ritz
Eàsula Sedlmaier
Samantha Sweetwater
Scott Watrous

The New Feminine Evolutionary:
Embody Presence—Become the Change

Sisterhood of the Mindful Goddess: How to Remove Obstacles, Activate
Your Gifts, and Become Your Own Superhero

Path of the Priestess: Discover Your Divine Purpose

Sacred Call of the Ancient Priestess:
Birthing a New Feminine Archetype

Rise Above: Free Your Mind One Brushstroke at a Time

Menopause Mavens: Master the Mystery of Menopause

The Power of Essential Oils: Create Positive Transformation in Your
Well-Being, Business, and Life

Self-Made Wellionaire: Get Off Your Ass(et), Reclaim Your Health, and
Feel Like a Million Bucks

Oms From the Mat: Breathe, Move, and Awaken to the
Power of Yoga

Oms From the Heart: Open Your Heart to the Power of Yoga

The Four Tenets of Love: Open, Activate,
and Inspire Your Life's Path

Visit us at floweroflifepress.com

Made in the USA
San Bernardino, CA
28 December 2018